T0195652

STREET FIGHTER

KEVIN GREEN

authorHOUSE®

AuthorHouse™
1663 Liberty Drive
Bloomington, IN 47403
www.authorhouse.com
Phone: 1 (800) 839-8640

Published by AuthorHouse 07/24/2018

ISBN: 978-1-5462-4924-5 (sc)
ISBN: 978-1-5462-4923-8 (e)

Library of Congress Control Number: 2018908062

Print information available on the last page.

Train and train to win (Time + Practice) = Greatness in skill

One must find greatness within, nothing is perfect including me. Life creates failure to exercise the mind and body for success. This is why practice creates perfection and self-meaning. One should always train to be ones best. Stay in control of the situations that lie ahead taming the dragon within to better increase ones chance of success especially when ones anger, and aggression is at its highest, to overcome ones inner demons and fears to win the battles that lie within to win and overcome the many obstacles and opponents that may come. Before ones demons and fears overpower ones state of mind. Control the dragon that lie within. No one is perfect this is why we train our minds and bodies to function. Progress is everything and survival is the key to life. (Like the old saying goes practice makes perfect).

Balance training and finding ones inner balance

Practice stance transfer from foundation to foundation, leg a to leg b. Practice standing, and find balance in the body starting at the foundation of the body. Standing on one leg and notice the location of the balance in the foot used to stand at all times, and understand the feel of balance while standing.

Learn how to manipulate one's body to move and bend at will.

Learn how to manipulate your opponent's body at will.

Practice locking an opponent's limb when your opponents on guard or off balance. Throwing an opponent off balance when in a match can be a great help when defending self.

Sometimes in life one has to lose many times before one can win. Don't let losing get in the way of progress. Life taught me losing makes one stronger and helped me gain a better understanding of life, greater experience in motion and the knowledge to win.

When transferring energy one shouldn't stop at the end of the action, follow through and let the energy flow through the body in the direction of the action, giving the action the amount of energy needed to produce success in the time provided or given becoming a part of one's actions combined with the actions from ones opponent.

Train to be able to use your environment to your advantage molding to every situation able to transform self to fit the situation at hand at any given time in the space provided. Any tool can be used to help preserve one's life and the lives of others if used correctly.

To be able to win in the time provided you have to know when to take advantage of the time giving, when to make a move, and how to take advantage of the opponent or opponents actions at any given time to ensure ones safety during training, sparing and especially during battle or combat.

Friendly and unfriendly sparing can and will greatly improve one's training. Learning how to overcome one's ego, and one's opponent deep inside the realm of one's opponent, inside their circle, molding to fit every situation. Each motion, action and technique can be completed differently becoming unique depending on the stance and method of motion, creating adaptation in motion allowing self to adapt to each new movement.

Sometimes in order to check ones progress you have to step back from the situation you're in and take a look at reality and understand life in a different light, form, and fashion. Calculate for the solution to the whole situation and plan and proceed with understanding.

Train for speed, agility and focus to create a greater external, and internal powers

Usually it's best to start at the base or foundation keeping ones balance bringing ones power from the base of the body or foundation moving the energy through the body feeling the transfer of energy until the time of release, letting the transfer of energy happen naturally. Flow through with ones action though the snap of the action feeling the release of energy. Then bring the energy back into one's self as one stays in a comfortable and constant position prepared for whatever action or actions that may come. (Learn the feel of the transfer of energy to maximize ones power).

To raise the bodies total strength (power) requires a great amount of practice and continuous exercise. Lots of repetitions using light or heavy weights building the body to perfect each action in the time provided while training the mind to remain calm, focused and most important relaxed with a constant and steady mental frame of mind. (This will increase ones total body strength).

Maintain total body flexibility internal and externally to better the body's ability to complete each action with swiftness, calmness, accuracy, and with great power to maximize one's ability to complete each action with ones total body strength.

One should keep ones tools sharpened for life and what life brings, self-defense, and combat when combat and self-defense is needed to better help preserve life. One should always hold the preservation for life in high regards to protect self and others, making sure never to misuse ones power for the incorrect reasons. When dealing with great power this will be harder then it seems one must always train to control the use of one's power internally and externally. Most of the time its better just to avoid unwanted confrontation, then to cause a problem or confrontation. Making sure when dealing with great power one must first learn great control.

I once hurt someone I truly love (uncontrolled misuse of one's power), and after that incident my life fell apart, I couldn't forgive myself and the one I hurt wouldn't forgive me, but it is up to that person to forgive me for my uncontrolled unwanted actions! As a result of my own actions that day and the mistake I made, I broke my right hand for hurting another. I had to live with what one has done, hoping and praying for one's forgiveness. Since then I have found a new form of inner peace still longing for love lost to violence. One should first learn great control to control to guide and control the great power within, without control one remains too wild. Learn to control the beast and greatness will follow.

Building a great weapon:

To form a great weapon out of the body requires much time and pain dulling the nerve endings in the skin producing calluses like the callus hand of a farmer or black smith, making sure not to cause too much injury in the hands, mind or body this requires much time to master. There are many methods to achieve a higher level of hardness like continuously hitting a hard surface like a wooden board over time this will change the body, and the body will adopt to this severe training, making it easier in time to complete this action with much less pain. One must be careful, this training can cause great damage to the body after time if one doesn't train safely. Make sure to train smart and carefully to increase to wellbeing of ones total being. Punching pads will help lessen the damage done to the body during training, and in time the experience from using the punching pads will increase ones power, speed, accuracy, timing, and strength. Additional weights can always be added to an exercise to increase the speed and power while training the muscles to complete the actions with added weight. Find ways to lessen the pain if possible while training to decrease the amount of pain felt. The idea is to train the body to complete each action for self-defense and or combat.

(So much to learn) stay focused!!

Building the body for speed requires much training time and dedication and many repetitions. The more reps done the faster one will become. Training the body to memories each action and complete each action with great speed requires a great deal of training. (Practice, Practice, Practice). Speed training while using a beat to keep track of each movement on and off beat is a very helpful attribute while building great speed within and throughout one's body preparing the eyes, body, and mind use to the timing of objects and obstacles. Using music or even the sound of running or dripping water can increase the strength of one's mental rhythm. The rhythm of sounds made from the energy added to a punching bag or punching pad will grant one the ability to strike an object at any given time with great speed. Listening and learning from the sounds of life will always teach valuable lesson to help open the many doors of life. Adding weights when one is ready will help build greater speed and once the weights are lifted after much needed training one will gain a greater understanding of what true strength can be. There are no limit, there are no boundaries find the falsehood within the limits and boundaries of life and free yourself from slavery. Find the problems and troubles that burden, break them down and set yourself free. Break one's own limits and boundaries and dissolve them with hard work and progress to better ones self mentally and physically and find new limits and new boundaries to overcome and melt away.

Usually you can find a breaking point at the center of an object. Stay focused, and focus on one point while focusing on everything else that surrounds, to better see and feel ones surroundings. The ability to understand the location of a common breaking point takes much time and practice to obtain the skills necessary to complete the action or actions.

Sitting in a crossed or uncrossed leg position focusing on nothing else except breathing. Focusing the eyes, and mind on one spot one point like a camera lens or a beautiful picture being able to see one object and the whole picture at the same time, expanding the limits of the eyes, and mind. Finding ones blind spots training the eyes one at a time to focus on targets or obstacles, (candles or any other light sources can be used in this type or style of training. Stay focused, blinking can cause one to lose a match, or life in a life or death situation. Practice to win and be very careful not to burn the cornea of the eye and after this training exercise, take time to rest the eyes to keep them from over working. Without the ability to see makes self-defense almost impossible unless one has trained one's body and mind to defend oneself without the ability of sight.

When throwing a punch, kick, or any other action, make sure the blow is centered and correct. Follow through with the action and snap after the target like a whip that curves around a tree following the flow of energy through the target.

While training with open eyes train to stay out of the line of danger at all times, this is very important especially when training to be untouchable in the opponent's realm.

Sometimes you just have to wait until your opponent gives you the opportunity and when the window of opportunity opens take full advantage of the moment and situation to remain successful. Timing plays a great factor in deciding the victor in close range hand to hand combat training to remain focused and alert at all times.

While training sparing fighting, or just while living everyday life dealing with the stress and strain of everyday life. Train the mind and body to remain in a calm and relaxed state of mind and try to ease the strain on the mind and body by finding peace and balance. Stress and strain uses vital energy, be careful when training so one doesn't cause too much damage to self or ones sparring partner.

Usually it's better to walk away from an unwanted situation or confrontation rather than to harm or more importantly be harmed unless no other choice is giving. Think carefully when making decisions when dealing with life and self-defense. (One must live with ones choices ones made). It is always better to build up as much positive karma as possible keeping in mind no one is perfect while every is trying to reach perfection. One can reach perfection by breaking down the falsehood of limitation and reaching new heights with practice and more practice. (Progress makes perfect).

One should move at one's own pace, one's own beat unless molding to another beat. Be yourself and choose your own path unless guided by a righteous positive force. To better find self and one's own beat, one must first find one's self and learn one's self inside and out, the boundaries and limits positive and negative parts of self in order to breakdown one's mental and physical boundaries and limitations to continue to constantly making progress.

Usually combat doesn't have a game plan so it is best for one to blend in with each new situation prepared and ready for the next action or situation to arise. Stay ready for anything that may occur, with a steady, calm, and constantly relaxed state of mind. Relax and focus on ones goals and control ones anger and aggression practice this daily on the search to find one's own perfection. (Hard work + Dedication + Time) = Progress. Keep training in time your hard work will pay off.

(Time + Dedication + Practice) = Skill

(Skill + Training + Time) = Experience

(Skill + Experience + Time) = Greatness

All progress is great progress.

One should take action and bring your ideas to life.

(Idea + Want + Action) = Progress

When possible make training as fun as possible depending on what one is training for. Life is too serious, one should enjoy life as much as possible. Make time for yourself and get to know yourself like the back of your hand, self likes and dislikes etc. (Simplicity is Genius).

(The idea is to become whole, to become one, to find self).

Seeing is believing, but one can't believe everything one sees or hears to be true. This is the time to separate reality from fiction. Keep your mind focused, calm, and clear. Find a state of focus while training the mind and body to locate what's wanted, unwanted, or desired and the ability to be able to tell the difference.

Zoning a state of mind where everything moves much slower in the mind's eye while concentrating on everything, seeing ones target or obstacle with the clearest of vision, staying completely focused on the target like it was in front of you right under your nose. Stay sharp and sharpen each tool to complete its function. Use your head when all else fails keep in mind (Mind over Matter) when training or defending oneself there is no pain, just what is and what isn't. In vital situations one can't afford to let pain be the cause of defeat.

(NO PAIN NO FEAR IN THE EYES OF THE ENEMY).

Fingertip pushups to build the necessary muscles in the hand, arms, chest and back overall strengthening the grip and frame. Once the hands and fingers are strong enough, more techniques will become possible. Learn how to walk on hands to increase the upper body's strength and to better guide one's body in finding ones balance at a different level. It's best to build greater hand and finger strength especially when weapons training. If one can't hold one to one's weapon, what good is the weapon? Weapons are very useful when trained properly, increasing eye and body coordination.

Helpful fun exercise and great game, using a ball connected to a string and practice throwing the ball and then pulling the ball back on the string by pulling the string toward self. This is a very effective exercise to train the body and eye's (hand and eye coordination) similar to a you you. Feel the stretch of the string, the weight and balance of the ball and the string and have fun.

Numbing or dulling the nerve ending in the skin and/or limbs can be done by continuously hitting a punching bag or pad, or any other hard or soft surface (very important) try your best not to break or damage any limbs or bones. The human body is very fragile and bones break very easily under extreme pressure. Unwanted breaks to the body makes training much harder because of the damage caused to the body. (Mind over matter)

(There is no pain until one can afford to feel) adrenaline will help the body relieve pain while in combat and / or training to lessen the amount of pain felt. This is where controlling anger and aggression comes in to play.

(Time + Anger + Aggression + Skill + Control) = Self control

Energy never stops, energy flows onward to different areas of life like the natural circle of life. Plants become food for animals and then animals become food for plants and so on. In life one can make a choice sometimes to choose which direction ones energy will flow. Eyes can only see what is, usually the eyes will only see what they believe to be true. Eyes can sometimes be deceiving sometimes one must use other senses to determine what is or isn't true, real or unreal. Especially when dealing with life and the preservation of life (Self Defense).

Life law number one: Self Preservation, protection of self and the protection of others, trying never to put self or anyone else in the eye of danger.

Train self to maintain an untouchable state and state of mind by staying out of the range of an opponent and/or one's enemy or enemies until the time of contact and location of target, and once one's target or opponents in range take action until the treat is gone. When ones mind and body is ready trust self while in motion, and make sure your actions are a solution to your problem. Learn to feel the moment of action, blend in with the opponent molding to their actions and solve the problem with moments that create peace and harmony.

Brust Punching and or kicking: Once one has committed ones self to take action in a sparing match or in the heat of battle. Once one starts the flow of energy one shouldn't stop the flow of energy until the threat and/or danger has been dealt with. Release as much energy needed while sparing and as much as possible when one's life is threatened. This way of thinking will give your opponent less time to cause any harm to self or loved ones. Release as energy to your opponent as possible, when possible to increase the chance of success and survival. Once the flow energy has settled and the threat has been dealt with one can go back to the ready position, returning to an untouchable state ready to perform another action and/or technique.

Never forgetting what one has done, in case one has to handle this problem and/or threat again.

Never forgetting what one has done, in case one has to handle this problem and/or threat again. Like they say **(It's always better to be safe than sorry)** especially in the eyes of the enemy. **(Safety first and foremost decreasing the chance of danger and/or dangerous situations).**

One's goal is to remain in an **untouchable state** when dealing with any form of combat to lessen the chance of injury and/or danger in or around the circle of one's opponent or opponents, staying out of the line of danger as much as possible. If your opponent can't reach you, then your opponent can't touch you, this lessens the chance of danger and dangerous situations. This **untouchable state** will also more importantly create peace without the constant threat of danger. **(Train body and mind to remain untouchable in the realm of one's opponent and/or enemy and/or enemies).**

When in combat ones whole body should move as smooth as an ice skater gliding smoothly over ice, with the power of an elephant capable of pushing over the biggest tree. Movements should be smooth flowing together with the correct balance at all times to increase the chance of winning. One must learn their yin and yang and find one own balance in every movement. **(Train to feel the balance outside and inside the whole)**. Without the correct balance one will fall increasing the chance of failure.

Every action flows smoother with the correct balance, as one completes the action. One shouldn't panic during hand to hand combat, and more importantly one shouldn't show fear in the eyes of the enemy and/or enemies. Opponents are more likely to attack when **fear** and/or **weakness** has been shown. **(Show no Fear, Show no Weakness)**.

Mind must be clear, calm remaining in ones relaxed state, cool like a running stream until one turn hard as ice, cooled by the winters chill focusing on one's opponent and/or action and actions of one's self focusing on self and opponents speed power strength and accuracy, timing and distance when one is in the realm of one's opponent and/or enemy. In order to hit or be hit one must be able to touch or be touched.

Train to remain in an untouched stated as often as possible when in the realm of the enemy. One should only strike when one heart is truly into the action, acting at the correct time, in the correct amount of space with the exact amount of power to give life to one's action letting the energy flow through ones target. In order to score a point one has to make a point happen when in a sparring match and/or battle with the full intention of winning knowing the feeling of lose in the back of one's mind.

Carrying, concrete, water, pebbles, sand, or dirt is a great workout to help build the body and enjoy the fresh air outdoors. Fill buckets weighing as much as you can carry without harming yourself, and carry the buckets from one place to another adding stairs or some other type of elevation changing the amount of resistance, building good muscle getting the body ready to carry out other actions and/or techniques to better guide your body in close range hand to hand combat. Don't stop, your muscles will adapt to the stress and strain after a while, and then add more weights to your exercises to increase the intensity. This type of training will also help build ones sense of balance as the weight shifts from side to side feeling the weight shift and keeping ones balance at the same time while walking back and forth. This is a great cardio exercise building both the upper and lower body at the same time. While performing this exercise try to concentrate on something other than the exercise to lessen the pain of lactic acid build up. This will help ease the pain mentally (**Mind over Matter**) remember there is no pain only results, no fear only results, (**Remember to eat and rest when performing these strenuous exercises and never exercise to the point of death or unbearable pain**). Some pain from lactic acid build up is ok and excepted, but the point is to exercise tone and build muscle not to kill yourself. (**Very important safety first**). Train the mind and body and reprogram the brain to carry out these training functions and/or routine.

Anger and **Aggression** can be very helpful in self-defense and combat as long as one control one's self control the inner beast that lays dormant inside all of us, and direct it towards opponent and/or enemy or enemies breaking their state of untouchable ness, bringing the transfer of energy from ones foundation flowing into and through opponent, and then bringing the energy back into one's own body keeping ones balance throughout the action and energy transfer.

$$(\text{Anger} + \text{Aggression} + \text{Control}) = \text{Controlled Aggression}$$
$$(\text{Time} + \text{Dedication} + \text{Practice}) = \text{Skill}$$

Mentally and psychically find the distance from each point of pivot, the distance from ones foundation to the end of each limb, getting to know the distance between you and your opponent, knowing how far and how long it will take to touch your opponent pushing your energy outward and then reeling this energy back into one's self.

Train for Speed: When speed training one should practice with very high repetitions to increase the ability to move at high speeds training mind and body to move quickly reprogramming the body and mind. Repeating the same action over and over again, each time getting faster in mind and body learning one's body, learning ones speed, and learning ones strength, and one's ability. Repeating the same action until the action becomes part of self <u>mentally</u> and <u>psychically</u> and even <u>emotionally</u>, until the action becomes natural, thus becoming part of self. Once the body and mind becomes use to this action one can then add weight to this action to increase the amount of strain to better build ones muscles, and to better build one's body and mind. Once the weight has been lifted the body will feel free and your body will be able to flow in time with your thoughts and actions, repeating the same action with all limbs and total body to increase ones total body speed. Practice speed training with and out beat, in and out of rhythm learning ones spirit becoming one with one's soul.

<u>Burst punches and kicks</u>: Punching and kicking until the limbs are too heavy to move (**Maxing out the kicking and punching muscles**). Once this gets easier for the body to handle add weights to the exercises to increase ones strength and power, always being careful not to harm one's self, moving incorrectly can cause great damage to one's body.

Before not to injury the joints maintaining total body balance through each exercise from start to finish. Ease the mind and concentrate on the target and/or targets until the match or battle is won are over.

(Clear the mind + Focus of ones skill + Use of great technique) = Ones best

Training for Power external and internal:

Building strength usually working with light or heavy weights and body weight building ones external power. Weight training in many different ways training the muscles to handling the amount of weight used, keeping this weight balance at all times using many different methods of lifting whatever works for you as long as you get the job done that's all that matter as long as you smart and safe about it. Working with sand, gravel, dirt, water, iron, steel, are even just normal body weight to gain stronger muscle mass. You can even use water resistance and then adding weights to this training program, water resistance is great for the joints and body because of less stress and strain to the muscles while at the same time building muscles. One must be very careful when dealing with water training so one doesn't drown are cause bodily harm One should never put one's life in jeopardy, protecting self and defending one's self is what Self Defense is all about protecting one's life at all times. Weight lifting starting with low weight until the body grows accustom to the stress and strain of the weight, and then move up in weight class until it is time to move up again in weight class building strong flexible tone muscle. One should always remember to give the muscles, body and mind a chance to rest once the body and mind become overworked or burnt out from the stress and strain of these hard strenuous exercises **(Mind over Matter)**. Keep strong in the body and mind with high spirits, and overcome the physical pain and mental pain and torcher that one goes through when building one's mind and body to complete these strenuous tasks, to reach a higher level of self and self-want, reaching higher levels internally, externally, mentally, and physically to surpass one's self and to become more than self. Keep a strong base usually in the ankles and feet, finds ones balance and maintain this balance throughout this function unless one using a different base for an action for **example**: the base of the arm is the chest, back and, shoulder which is the foundation for the arm. Make sure to make each movement as smooth as possible to better maintain ones balance. When one muscle or group of muscles become too tired or (burnt out) or (maxed out) to continue one should exercise a different muscle and/or muscle group or a different exercise and/or technique until ones muscles heals and is capable to complete its function again. A healthy diet will be very helpful in rebuilding the muscles and fueling the body to complete each action. **(Find <u>Chi</u> the <u>true meaning</u> and feel of <u>Chi</u> strength in the flow of great energy)**. Let the energy flow like a running stream, like the rotation of the world, calm like a mirrored lake or a pleasant summer's day flowing like the winds timeless and constant living in forever ness.

In order to live life one has to experience life. If you don't live life than how would you know what life feels like, the taste of cool water on a hot day, the smell of breakfast waking one up to the smell great food and life, memorizing the smell of the spring and fall the feel of snow under ones warm feet in winter. The feel of love and love lost. The hurt from lose are losing a loved one. **(One should experience life and what life brings, and <u>hopefully</u> life brings more great things than unwanted life experiences)**. Living life requires lots of hard work, but like can also be great fun when you appreciate what life is and what life isn't appreciating the little amount of time that we are given. Like my mother told me when I was growing up **(Life isn't Fair)** bad things happen to great people all the time and great things happen to bad people and vice versa. I'm not the one to judge you, are anyone else I'm too busy living my life trying my best to enjoy this life until my life comes to an end appreciating everything and every breath that accompanies me in this short life that I live. The good things we look forward to, and the bad things we learn from appreciating it all as one maintaining or trying to maintain a calm, relaxed pleasant state and state of mind excepting myself as a whole being excepting myself as one, and always keeping my human nature in mind staying true to self and self-kind. You don't need to touch fire to feel the heat, but sometimes one must touch the fire to learn that the heat from the flame will, and can burn.

One must be true to self in order to be true to someone else. Respecting one's life and the life of others and hopefully others will respect one's self, and remember that nothing in life is fair and nothing in life is guaranteed. But if one tries to live life with honor, loyalty, truthfulness, and respect for self and others hopefully it will pay off and you will live and life full of greatness receiving what is given.

Except one's self and ones faults and flaws as one, one can try to fix ones flaws if possible if ones flaws are even flaws at all. Learning from each mistake trying not to reproduce these faults excepting one's self as whole excepting one's self as one correcting what is unwanted and living with what's wanted practicing to become one's own perfection. Practice makes perfect or close to it. (**Train to be ones best at all times and remember very important no one is perfect but one can reach one's own perfection if one wishes ones best is ones perfection**).

The idea behind **self-defense** is to protect not harm, to be as strong as the suns light and as gentle as the summer's wind, to save one's self not to harm self or someone else this is my definition of self-defense.

When training one should control ones anger and aggression by channeling ones anger and aggression inward keeping ones balance a calm mind staying as relaxed as possible keeping control, then once one is ready to release this energy outward focusing this energy towards ones target rather it be an opponent or punching pad or punching bag, control the release of this energy never letting it build up too much this will cause an unwanted action releasing this energy in the wrong place and at the wrong time, the body and mind can only take some much and when the fire or energy get to much or too high it will find a release so it's best to channel this energy that lies within into a controlled action like hitting a punching bag, running, jogging, yelling, singing writing, find some way to release this anger, this aggression to keep from harming one's self and others this is the way I release my own anger and aggression, sometimes just walking outside and even better going for a joyride in the car, doing anything to release this unwanted anger and aggression to keep this power from harming self and others, this requires a great deal of practice and is very possible if you want to keep from harming self and others. Meditation is another great form of release calming the mind, body and spirit, almost anything is better than harming one's self and others. **(Energy + Skill) = Great Power** that must **be controlled to maintain** one's life and the life of others, and remember that one is responsible for one's action and should ones best not to cause actions one doesn't believe in or action that are uncalled for. There is always somebody better, there is always somebody stronger there is always somebody father ahead, knowing this concentrate on one's ability not the ability of others knowing that one can train to raise or lower one's ability and/or power to a different level, knowing this become self and train to be ones best **(Practice makes Perfect)** or one's own perfection just be yourself. **(Be as Good or as Great as one can become or even better in time with much training and practice).**

Anger and Aggression sometimes fuels the body and mind releasing adrenaline fueling increasing ones power and strength. Controlling this extra amount of power takes much time, practice, patients, dedication and much skill always depending on one's emotional state and state of mind. When dealing with anger and aggression it's always best to keep a clear and opened frame of mind to solve the problem and/or problems that one is dealing with at the time. To make the correct and just action not causing a problem when trying to solve a problem should be ones goal. One shouldn't take action for the wrong, incorrect, and unjust reasons. One shouldn't cause a problem when trying to solve a problem this doesn't solve ones problem, this isn't the solution to one's problem. When one want or needs to solve a problem he or her should know the entire problem to make the correct and just action. One should have the correct problem and the correct variables to the problem to solve ones problem so one doesn't create new problems. Maintain focus and a calm state of mind to lessen the stress and strain and one's heart rate, too much stress and strain can cause heart attacks and seizures among many other harmful diseases.

In close range hand to hand combat train to be able to tell the difference between friend and foe so one doesn't harm someone that doesn't have to do with the altercation. One doesn't want to harm a friend when defending oneself, a friend should never be an intended target when dealing with hand to hand combat unless one is training and/or sparing with a friend. Keep one's eyes open focusing on the intended target and/or targets. Practice locating a few targets focusing on all targets, while planning the attack like a game of chess, choosing the correct moves for the correct time and timing the each target so one know how and when to act. Train to feel the moves of your opponent and plot a course of action moving a few steps ahead of the match in case your opponent throws a blow or blocks ones action evades ones actions or counters ones actions, this will enable you to take action without thinking, feeling the movements of both self and opponent or opponents in very little time. **(Remember that all progress is good progress as long as you make progress in one's action even if one has to take two steps back to take three steps forward.)**

Another great exercise for the body, many repetitions of pushing and pulling heavy objects with the hands, palms, back, and shoulders to build the correct muscles to complete different techniques to perform in sparing matches and self-defense. Using a rope to pull the object from one point to another, using the arms, back, and legs muscles to complete this task. Pushing the object with ones fists, palms, legs, and shoulders to increase the amount of force that can be applied at any given time and/or place and overall strengthen the body to complete different and more advance techniques. This type of training requires much practice, time, physical strain, dedication, and pain from lactic acid build up. Many repetition are needed so one can grow accustom to the physical pain that these exercises cause, and one must be very careful not to harm one's self moving this heavy load. Be careful and keep your body a good distance for the obstacle so the object doesn't fall over on you or fall on someone or something else. (Practice makes perfect results will come and you will soon empress yourself don't give up)!!!

(Train smart, and remember safety first, if you have problems moving this heavy weight then start at a lower weight and then build your mind and body until your body can handle the load.)

Leverage plays the biggest factor when dealing with close range hand to hand combat. You must be flexible, able to bend the match and/or situation to your favor. Balance plays a crucial role in gaining leverage in close range hand to hand combat; usually the one with the most amount of leverage wins the match unless one is just outmatched letting one gain the upper hand. Usually in a real altercation the one who hits first wins unless the opponent breaks the rhythm of the attack, usually one doesn't stop hitting until the fight or match is over dealing with burst hitters or burst throwers. In a match or a hand to hand altercation usually once the blows are thrown they shouldn't stop until the match or altercation is over, using the correct techniques to protect one's self and to end the altercation as soon as possible, if one is going to defend one's self one should do what one need to in order to win or escape with the less amount of harm done to self and opponent, keeping respect for self and life in mind at all times. Learn how to read your opponent or opponents with great amount of detail, and react before they react, respond before they respond. Learn your space and your opponent's space to better the chance of success in almost any situation and take advantage of the time given by opponent, opponents and/or self.

How long can one win? (Be the best you can be, continue to make progress and don't limit yourself or stunt self-growth. Be boundless and anything is possible).

(Simplicity is next to genius) Simply if one can't be touched then one is untouchable, one can only be touched when one is touched.

Never enter a battle or match knowing victory, tides change very quickly and ones outcomes is never really known. One should never underestimate ones opponent, or one will give ones opponent the upper hand and advantage during the match or battle, one might meet an unwanted and/or unplanned or unseen attack. Keep your eyes on your opponent or opponents opened and focused on your opponent or opponents reading their every movement and plan your defense action or offensive action an take action once ones time is just and correct, acting with speed, power, and extreme accuracy letting ones energy flow into and through the opponent or opponents. **(Muscle tension helps when looking for an opponent's next move, waiting for the muscles to flex watching and waiting for the time to defending one's self. Little tale tail sign that help when looking for an opponent's action of quick release or opening in opponents defense).**

(Eyes open and focused on the prize at all times).

(Ones foundation should be rooted strong and sturdy to hold one together).

Sometimes it's not the action but what happens after the action ones consequence that matters must. Hoping never to act in an incorrect or in just manner, stay focused and aware of ones environment with a clear, calm, and relaxed mental frame of mind. Find the beat to self and then find the beats to one's environment and/or situation to better blend in with one's environment and/or situation this will enable you to make better actions when ones becomes part of the whole when one really and truly becomes one.

Better to say sorry for disrespecting someone and ask for forgiveness rather than have the situation and/or altercation turn into a battle or life threatening situation. It's always better to control ones anger and aggression than to let the problem escalate to a greater problem that could potentially become life threatening and have the problem overwhelm oneself. Its best to keep a clear, calm, focused, and relaxed state of mind to keep unwanted confrontation and problems from happening to one's self. Don't let ones pride or ego get in the way of relationships or what is and what isn't, look at the problem are situation at hand for what the situation is or isn't, this will should give you the information you need to make the correct and just decision to solve ones problem. **(One should control ones great power and strength mentally, physically, and spiritually before ones power and strength controls the one that is in control.)**

When ones back is against the wall one has actually closed a few lines of danger, now knowing which direction the danger will be sent from. When ones back is against the wall a few lines of danger have already been closed so ones back is safe from danger, now one has to protect ones front from danger but one has less room to maneuver not being able to move in the backwards direction, so actions must be quick and swift with a great amount of timing to increase success in the mist of danger. When possible use your opponent's weight, force, and balance against them putting the leverage of the altercation in ones favor increasing the chance of success. One shouldn't fight a fight or battle one can't win unless given no other choice. One should also search for peace inside of an altercation if at all possible to increase the chance of survival and success in self-defense and the protection of oneself and others controlling the power within.

Build one's body and mind for speed, agility, balance, strength, power, and wisdom to better oneself and to make other more advanced techniques possible.

Usually if you beat the biggest majority usually the rest will fall or fall back to reorganize their plans or plan of attack, giving one time to reevaluate ones next plan or plan of attack planning how to deal with the rest of ones enemies and/or opponent and/or opponents. Acting with a clear and clam strong mind to take care the rest of ones opponents or opponents, never underestimating ones attacker or attackers keeping in mind that they mean you harm and will usually do almost anything to harm one. Keep one's mind and eye open ready to blend in and mold to one's situation and attackers. **(Stay completely focused when one is in (Fight Mode) and try your best to stay untouchable in the realm of one's enemy)**. Keep balance throughout each action and focus on your attacker, attackers, and/or targets at all times to increase one chance of success and to increase one survival.

Learn ones Flower (range of motion) each limb has its pivot and different foundations for each limb, find each limb's boundaries and limits and range of motion for each limb to increase success when training to make an offensive plan of attack. (**There is no action until there is action**)

Learn self totally and fully, learn ones likes, dislikes, and what feel comfortable to self to increase the happiness of one's life fix what is fixable and don't worry about the thing in one's life that one can't fix or change and never limit self. One should find ones limits and then break them down, if one can't reach the top now, then one should train to reach the top, if one needs help to reach the top then one should find help, and one should never take advantage of oneself or others in the wrong fashion maintaining peace between self and others, one shouldn't ask something of someone knowing that one wouldn't do what one ask that someone to do maintaining a constant circle of **good karma**. One shouldn't let pride or one ego make one feel ashamed from asking for help when help is needed. (**Break down the limits that lie within self and find one, one must understand self so one can understand life (one meaning one as a whole not partial)**).

Life is bitter and sometimes sweat and always ever changing leaving one the time and chance to find one's self it is usually up to the one that is living one's life to choose which path or paths to take, the choice is usually there if you can look inside yourself mentally and spiritually to understand oneself. Focus on progress in life, progress make progress until progress makes perfect or ones perfection. Don't let yourself get in the way of self or self-progress. Find a path or course of action and stay steady in the mind body and spirit to reach ones goal or goals. We have very little time to live considering the time span of life and time, we must choose wisely before we choose unwisely. We can't live without life or what life brings.

Everyday life outside of battle and self-defense should be as pleasant and pleasing as possible remembering to keep a clear, and calm mind with a relaxed state of mind learning from experience and what one has experienced making as much progress in life and life's goals to help keep one spirits as high as possible bring hope and possibility to one's life and hopefully the lives of others. **Meditation** also can help sooth one's self in the body and mind, sitting in a dim or dark room letting the mind and body relax, while the mind clears its self and calms oneself to better take on one day helping one bring ones anger and aggression down as low as possible creating peace and tranquility within one's self, separating oneself even if just for a few brief moments for the stress and strain of ones sometimes hectic life and life style helping one remain self.

Try not to let anyone or anything take you out of comfort and/or your relaxed state and state of mind training the mind and body to remain calm especially when ones anger and aggression becomes heighten, sometimes just walking away or redirecting ones attention can help in the success of reaching this peaceful, calm, relaxed state, and state of mind. Try to find peaceful way to deal with ones who taunt, ones who try to take one's self out of one's peaceful and relaxed state of mind to solve an peaceful problems or unwanted situations when possible to keep the peace flowing. Remain cool, calm, and collective, cool like a running stream, keep your mind clear, running smooth and soothing like a smooth nicely woven piece of silk, capable of become as hard as iron or steal when one's life becomes in danger to maintain one's life and hopefully the lives of others, keeping this relax and calm state of mind and remaining focused as much as humanly possible for the preservation of one's life and the lives of others. Taking deep breaths to ease the mind and body helps in controlling ones anger and aggression making it easier for one to maintain their peaceful state of mine. The object is to gain control of self especially when one becomes or feels uncontrollable **Inner Peace.** Controlling one's self and one's inner energy, training to control the beast within us all, the inner animal that usually lies dormant inside waiting for release this is uncontrolled power unless one has trained one's self, self-control. Sometimes it's better to walk away from a situation than have the situation escalate causing harm to self or others. Focus on one's own life first and foremost before worrying about others one must first take care of oneself, one can't help others if one isn't here or available to help, this means one should take care of one's self body, mind, and spirit keeping one's self balanced and centered within one's life. When one is dealing with a problem or an unwanted situation one shouldn't let the problem win one should try ones best to solve and win walking away from the problem with the solution to one's problem living with answer staying in one's peace and peace of mind staying as relaxed as possible unless one has to control and channel one anger and aggression to protect one's life in self-defense.

To be the best one must first train to be the best or ones best making progress and taking step after step to meet and surpass ones goal or goals, never giving up on self and always when training giving ones best and ones best ability to increase the chance of obtaining ones goals. Knowing one's ability knowing ones limits and boundaries and learning self and eventually surpassing self-becoming one with self.

Vertical Pushups: While keeping your legs and feet pointed up with both hands on the ground maintaining this position as long as you can if possible or when possible slowly descend your body and then lift your body and total body weight up, repeat this action as many times as possible building strength and power in ones hands, arms, shoulders, chest, and upper and lower back. This exercise will also build ones full total body balance. If your muscles aren't strong enough to complete this exercise start with regular pushups or try using a wall or an exercising partner to carefully help you complete this and other exercises, always keeping in mind safety first and foremost to lessen the chance of injury to self and others. After finishing this exercise one should rise slowly to lessen the chance of fainting due to the changing of blood flow and the amount of oxygen feeding the brain. (**One should keep great body circulation good blood flow**).

Training drills keep a good pace while drill training

Side to Side stepping
This exercise is best done in an area that
Has enough room to carry out these
Exercises freely and without restriction.
From point A to point B running from side to
Side in a straight line while changing the leg in
Front while putting the other leg behind and
Repeating this action again and again building
Balance, strength and agility. Make sure each
Exercise is done properly and correctly without
The cause of injury to self.

Running Tires
Using tires running while stepping inside the
Tires starting at point A tire running until
Point B and then repeat this exercise in
Many repetition gaining speed, agility,
Strength, and power.

Box Jumping
Starting at point A ending at point B and
Starting over again doing as many repetition
As possible keeping balance and keeping the
Heart rate up letting the body sweat and letting
The muscles build up lactic acid to rip the muscles.

(When obstacle training it's very effective for agility, speed, quickness, and power getting the body and mind for techniques and self-defense always careful not to harm self when training.)

Jump rope is another great agility building exercise. Make sure that the jump rope is long enough but not too long so one can complete this exercise without harming self. Keep both legs inside the range of the rope and keep legs under the body to increase balance, take your time and time each jump when possible to better the success of each jump.

Keep your balance and keep a fluid motion going to keep the heart rate up. Focus on balance while in motion, while the balance in motion changes. Once one is better and this action becomes more fluid try jumping with one leg at a time alternating between legs.

Jumping drills for agility using one leg at a time keeping your balance on one leg the switching to alternate leg by jump kicking and then back to the first leg with a jump kick then repeating this exercise using the same and different kicks remaining balance and centers concentrating on one's target, a real target like a punching bag or imaginary space keeping ones balance throughout the exercise training the body and mind to move as one. This will help in gaining balance and agility, quickness and power burst punching and kicking and overall speed. When trying try to switch from one leg to the other as quick as possible like the game hot potato being swift with the feet spending most of the time practicing attack and switching of legs and other limbs. Have as much fun as possible training but train as hard as possible to receive the greatest amount of results. Train to become as perfect as one can become and then surpass one's self and ones limits reaching ones unmentionable goals and success hard training makes this all possible. (**Remember there are no limits, there are no boundaries like space there is always more of it if one can find it**).

Running and walking help in fitness a great deal building and toning muscle and raising ones metabolism helping the body burn fat and calories to help keep the body in shape, also running and walking helps in keeping and knowing ones balance keep track of where one hold ones balance and the shift of ones balance to better maintain ones balance. Also running and walking are great stress relievers taking the mind and body away from stressful situation and confrontations. Making sure to keep ones balance throughout each action, especially when one's making an action.

(**Hydration is key when training to fuel the body and mind to help cleanse the body of waste and toxin no matter what the situation**)

Make a mental note to stay inside ones state of relaxation unless one anger and aggression is needed in self-defense to protect and preserve one's life, maintaining ones untouchable state to increase the chance of success and to increase the chance of living with getting harmed and without harming anyone unintentionally or without cause preserving life should always be the answer. Staying in one's untouchable state until one enters and then defend self until one doesn't need to defend and then one should return to the state of untouchable ness once ones opponent has been taking care of.

(Fighting should be the last resort in self-defense and the preservation of life).

When dealing with self-defense manage the space between self and opponent while maintaining ones balance through **(total body balance).** Try to keep legs under the body at all times to better control ones balance, keep a sturdy and strong foundation throughout one's body the buttocks plays a great role in balance especially when flexed. Keeping the balance either on the heels of the feet or the balls of the feet to better manage ones balance while keeping a lower center of gravity with knees slightly bent to lessen the chance of losing one's balance during movements unless one has committed one's self to an action.

(Practice of technique + Weight + Repetition) = Building and Toning of muscle (Add more weight to increase muscle tone and muscle size).

Range of motion is very important in combat, flexibility helps to complete each action and to increase ones power within action. Starting the action from the base of one's foundation and letting the energy flow through and throughout and then back to the start of the action ready to produce another action if needed. Balance is always important in combat, self-defense, and everyday life and one's everyday lifestyle staying on ones feet as much as possible when defending one's self to increase the chance of success and remember practice makes ones perfection.

To remain untouchable or to remain in one's untouchable state in close range hand to hand combat, one must be able to maintain and control ones space and what lies within ones space, being able to keep ones opponent and/or enemy out of one's safety circle of one's untouchable realm. Once you commit to an action one shouldn't give ones opponent time to react this increases the chance of harm to self-one should defend self as much as humanly possible if one give an opponent time to react one might be harmed by an attack from ones opponent, remain in one's untouchable state to lessen the risk of harm. Build the body and mind and the tools of one's body for application of technique sharpened for self-defense and combat, practice using these tools forever ready to preserve one's life. Wooden man or Wing Chung dummies are great for practicing martial arts self-defense techniques helping one judge distance timing, speed, and power. **(Practice makes perfect).**

When maintaining your untouchable state it's very important to maintain ones space controlling one's mind and body controlling ones breathing at all times. Being aware of ones opponents space as well as ones opponents' actions and balance ready to avoid all actions and blows thrown into ones space increasing the chance of success. Once one is engaged in combat or action one should try to finish the altercation as soon as possible to reduce the amount of damage to self. Usually the quickest actions win unless ones action has been broken, stopped, or countered, if ones action has been broken, stopped, or countered produce another action to catch ones opponent and/or opponents off guard keeping the action going as much as possible giving ones opponent or opponents less time to react to ones actions. Closing the line of danger is vital when one is defending one's self, it doesn't matter how the line is closed or stopped as long as the action becomes none existent opening ones opponent to welcome ones action or actions when defending one's self, locating weak spots in ones opponents fighting style or form or fighting or combat stance always protecting ones vital areas at all times to decrease the amount of damage done to self by blocking, countering, or throwing of ones techniques, if one loses ones balance or is hit by an action react as soon as possible to preserve one's self when defending one's self. Keeping one's eyes on one's opponent or opponents at all-time waiting and watching for one's opponent or opponents next action or actions, remembering where ones opponent space lies at all times when possible and to decrease the chance of an opponent's hit to self, being able to speed up or slow down ones action to blend in with one's opponent or opponents making it easier to locate targets in opponents defense with the correct timing, speed, power, and accuracy unless one opponent is out of range in their untouchable state. Training to move in and out of one's opponent range and range of sight remain in one's untouchable state inside the realm of ones opponents space. Usually if your opponent can't see you then one has a better chance of success when defending one's self, locating your opponents blind spots and range of sight training the all the senses to help locate ones opponent especially when ones in the realm of one's opponent keeping track of their action and patterns of action to increase the chance of success planning ones moves of action and prediction the action of one's opponent figuring out there next move or moves like a game of chess **(Chess is a great game for the mind to learn strategic moves and actions)**. If ones opponent or opponents happens to land a blow or beats one in action try to push their energy plus the energy of self onto one opponent countering, increase the amount of energy released opening ones opponent getting ones opponent ready to receive action or action a or blow or combination of blows when defending one's self. Pushing an opponent off balance is another great way to avoid a blow or set action causing ones opponent to reset their balance and force of action balance plays the biggest factor in combat living in the realm of one's opponent. Sometimes the closest tool or weapon to one's opponent is ones shortest tool to transfer ones energy, this shouldn't be a problem if one trains and practices to strengthen ones whole and total body. Throwing off an unwanted action or attack by blocking or countering at the correct time opening up a new point of entry plays a vital role in offensive actions, and once one opens the door of entry try to stay inside the opening until one has successfully defended one's self, if one doesn't continue to act then ones opponent will have a better chance to cause one harm also ones opponent will have a better chance of blocking ones action or countering ones actions.

One should stay out of the line of danger when waiting for an opening in ones opponents defense to present its self, once the opportunity arises take full advantage of this moment to better defend one's self as soon as possible to lessen the risk of harm, one shouldn't hesitate when in combat defending one's self. Keep focused on opponent and ones targets to better the chance of success, completing each action in the time provided by ones opponent taking full advantage of one's time. Each action must be true to self while blending in with one's opponent and opponents actions until the confrontation or combat has been completed, staying focused at all times controlling ones anger and aggression channeling this controlled anger and aggression towards ones attacker while defending one's self and preserving one's life, focusing this energy with every weapon or tool needed to preserve one life, becoming one with self, opponent, and ones surroundings. (**Balance of control of self is the overall key to winning in self-defense). Most Important when learning how to defend one's self one must first and foremost learn <u>discipline</u>.** One should always remain careful when in fight mode one can get lost in the adrenaline and the rush of adrenaline being very addicting, this state of mind can cause great stress and strain to the body and mind using up vital body and mental energy, one must learn to know focus and control when dealing with fear, anger, and aggression as much as possible to lessen the effects on self, not holding on for too long, directing this energy into self and then outward in a peaceful manner unless defending one's self or dealing with self-defense, respecting self, life, pain and the lives of others while maintaining a clear and calm mental state of mind. (**Sometimes the answer you seek lies in the past, sometimes in the future, must of the time ones past makes ones future if one learns from ones past or the past of others).**

Another great exercise for total body balance and coordination great for the legs and foot coordination especially playing with or practicing with a very small bean bag the size of a lemon keeping eyes on the **bean bag** at all times, keeping the bean bag in the air by kicking it up every time it falls like a soccer ball which is also great exercise, try catching the bean bag with the feet and other parts of the body keeping the bean bag from hitting the ground this can be great fun as well as great exercise for the body and mind building total body balance and total body coordination. (**Play around with the bean bag by one's self or** others practicing techniques of all kinds being careful not to harm self or others while learning).

To learn self and one's body one must first learn self and how to use one's body, learning how to use one's body to perform wanted action and techniques. Learning ones range of motion and one's body limits, **learning ones flower (range of motion).**

Drinking hot liquids help to loosen the mucus in the throat and nasal pathway helping one to breath, also breathing in steam as long as the temperature isn't to high can help breathing to keep the body to better perform actions. (Be careful not to burn one's self keeping the steam at a safe temperature) also steam can be a great way to cleanse the pore in the skin removing toxins from the body.

When training with hard surfaces like a wood man or wing chug dummy to lessen the amount of presser or pain cause or felt enabling one to exercise for a longer period of time giving one more time to practice with less pain to the body, this type of training can be very hard on one's body depending on how hard one trains or how hard one hits. (**Be very careful when training self and especially when training others and remember all progress is great progress as long as one gets better and even better in time and if one runs into problems never let pride or ego get in the way of success unless a situation breaks ones moral code, no one's perfect but one can reach one's own perfection and then surpass one's own perfection**).

Sometimes one must let go of things to grip on something more valuable, if something is truly yours then one shouldn't be able to lose it, but if one does then usually one will find it again.

Always be true to self and self needs, it's very easy to lose one's self in one's own world forgetting what is fact and what is fiction one must be able to separate between the two and ultimately find what is real and what is real to self-finding ones balance within balance.

(**Hoping for the best and expecting the worst of self and others and** searching for and finding what is really true, every wave produced has a ripple and a consequence one must live with one's own action and even the actions of others).

One must remember to respect ones opponent and more importantly respect one's self never underestimating self or opponent but if one is going to underestimate someone make sure itself. Self-defense is for self-dense only unless dealing in a match or competition or tournament and in matches make sure one respects ones opponent not necessarily liking ones opponent but respecting the other half of ones match, respecting life keeping in mind that no one controls all and total power of all one can only truly control one's self and one's action usually unless one can't control one's self at all. Everything in life has a beat, find ones beat like the beat of one's heart and then one can focus on finding the beat to others, learn the feeling of one's own beat and become one with and within self, molding to life and what life brings step by step. Respecting ones energy and the energy left behind by others while expressing one's self and remembering that one's skill and one's life can and will come to an end, taking advantage of every breath and day that one is given until the end. **(Live life to the fullest, have fun be safe and make life worth meaning).**

Give ones opponent no time to make action, no space to react, close their circle with great speed, accuracy, strength and power with great timing.

(Ones weight and size doesn't play the biggest role in deciding the victor of combat usually the deciding factor has all to do with ones muscles and muscle mass, skill, experience and one's timing when dealing with self-defense close range hand to hand combat).

(Time + Dedication + Practice) = Skill
(Skill + Training + Time) = Experience
(Skill + Experience + Time) = Greatness

Locking limbs and joints of opponents will help to close some lines of danger stopping the action of the limb, opening up windows for action. Be careful when sparing with a sparring partner not to add too much pressure when training to lock limbs causing one opponent to break under pressure learn the feel of the limb locking learning the breaking point of each limb without breaking ones sparring partner so one doesn't harm ones partner and have to pay ones sparing partners hospital bill. **(Practice makes perfect accidents happen but try ones best not to break or harm ones friends).** Lock the joints and limbs by press up or down on one side or both sides of the limb or joint pushing the limb or joint the opposite way of the functioning joint or limb is supposed to move feeling the tension in the limb or joint knowing when the limb or joint is locked or not and if needed knowing how to break the limb or joint if needed when dealing with life threatening situations. Remember to protect one's self especially when one has committed to the action of locking limbs or joints creating opening in one's self-defense. This type of training can be very dangerous and painful and should only be used when in self-defense when one life is in jeopardy, one must learn control. **(If one is going to practice the locking of limbs and joints one must learn how to fix the bones in the limbs and joints in case of breaks are dislocation of the body learning the balance in self and life. Learn other methods of medication if possible to help relieve the body of pain and ailments and sickness to help maintain one's life. Learn pressure points and acupuncture if possible to help maintain life).**

Stretching helps in finding ones balance within self and throughout technique helping one learn ones range of motion and/or ones flower or sphere. Focus on the position of one's body and the surrounding area becoming one with ones surroundings, knowing the reach distance for each limb and how long it take for one to reach a point in ones surroundings knowing the time it takes to get from one point to another to increase the amount of knowledge of self-learning one's personal space.

Always keep hands and feet ready to apply action and technique training to be able to defend one's self at all time. Practicing to protect one's body whole and totally, training to avoid all attacks and being able to defend one's self in all situations to help preserve one's life, maintaining a constant visual on ones targets incase action is needed to defend one's self. Train the body and mind to act and make action without the sense of sight in case one has to defend one's self without the sense of sight or the ability to see are the inability to see ones opponent, using other senses to hone in on one's opponent feeling where the opponent is ready to take action to defend one's self without the sense of sight using the ears and sense of hearing to find ones opponent listening to the whereabouts of ones opponents footsteps and the sound of ones opponents body and limbs cutting through the air, feeling the force of wind against the body and face giving one tale tail signs of ones opponents whereabouts, smelling the breath of the opponent learning to tell where ones opponent is without being able to see. Protecting one's body and especially ones vital points to aid in the preservation of one's life ready to take action becoming one with ones opponent without the ability of sight when it really counts where inside the ring or inside the realm of one's opponent. **Meditation** helps when learning how to defend one's self without the sense of sight, **finding sight without sight** getting to know self when in the dark another world within a world when one meditates learning self and inner peace within self-clearing the mind and cleansing the spirit thinking of nothing at all clearing the mind or taking a trip within one's mind, this take much practice and concentration and focus helping one rid the body of stress, strain, and dedication helping one find one's self and **what makes one truly happy peace and inner peace. (Imagination holds the key to life; anything is possible if you put your mind to it).**

One should ask ones self-questions like if one is inside a dwelling or home, is one just self or is one a part of the whole meaning part of the dwelling or home? Can one be only one or can one become more than one? These are questions one should ask one's self to better find one's self and figure out the questions and answers to life.

Everything in life has a beat either becoming one with the beat of life or maintaining one's own beat, like the beat of the heart the pulse of the human body and the pulse and vibration of the earth and everything else, moving to the rhythm of life its self-feeling the vibration of life becoming one with life whether one realizes this to be true or not everything in life has a beat or vibration effecting everything in life like a ripple in a pond. If an earthquake causes a tree to fall and the tree then fall and lands on a home the beat of the earth and the vibration of the world is felt by that home and the contents in it causing the home and contents of the home and beings living in the home to feel the effect having to deal with the actions of the beat and vibration of the earth leaving the after affects to deal with soaking up the energy passes on by the world and surroundings. **(One should think about what actions one makes when deciding what actions to make).**

Throwing ones opponent can be very helpful in self-defense causing ones opponent to lose vital balance helping in self-defense taking ones energy and leverage away from the opponent and adding it to ones action by using the hips, should, legs, and arms to throw or push ones opponent away from self, in order to complete the action of throwing one must be in the realm of one's opponent finding ones balance and taking the balance from ones opponent by grapping ones opponent and using leverage to take ones opponent off their feet and then to the ground by force of self or the force of one's opponent, throws can be very dangerous and harmful to opponent so one should only use throws when practicing self-defense or defending one's self. **Tripping and sweeping** ones opponent can also play a great factor in defending one's self-taking ones opponent off balance giving one time to better defend one's self when ones opponent balance has been taking opening up ones opponent for other actions using ones total body to take the leverage away from ones opponent giving one more time to make actions when defending self.

Dodge ball is another great exercise helping one learn ones untouchable state gaining eye and body coordination speed and agility as one locating the direction of an object and knowing the line that which it travels training to avoid this line or line of danger remaining in one's untouchable state training the mind and body to avoid this line of danger without mind, and without thought. Dodge ball is a game played by usually more than one person, someone throwing the ball and someone dodging the ball taking turns once a player gets hit giving the other person a chance to throw or dodge the ball learning the different lines and angles and potential lines of danger, while having as much fun as possible learning as much as possible. Keeping mental notes of ones actions to increase the chance of success keeping ones balance at all times keeping one's self out of the lines of danger.

It takes more than one to raise a village, together we stand strong holding tight to our foundations, like the roots that keeps a tree standing tall, like a herd of elephants that protect the young in the center of the family group everyone pitching in to teach the whole group in order for better survival, teaching morals and the morals and rules to life.

(One can only learn so much, one can gain much more knowledge when one has the chance to gain knowledge from the whole bettering the chance of survival for all).

One should train to cut through air and space to reach ones target or opponent with great speed increasing ones timing and speed decrease the amount of surface area passing through the air and space. Speed drills will help aid in learning how to decrease the amount of one's surface area in action increasing the actions speed with less energy used, a thin object will cut through air faster than a flatter or wider object would, the thinner object taking less time to reach a point from start to finish practice this and learn the feel of one's surface area being able to reach much faster speeds practicing accuracy timing and focus increasing the chance of making contact with one's target or opponent on and off beat to fit ones situation. **(Always practicing to become better than one once was, bettering one's self).**

In order to live in peace, one must live a peaceful existence with a peaceful frame of mind hoping that one's aura and good karma rubs off on to others keeping the positive energy flowing increasing the peace and one's peaceful state, in order to remain in a peaceful state one should try ones best not to make enemies even though people hate people sometimes for no reason at all, usually because of something that happen or didn't happen to them trying to find a release for their negative energy without harming themselves by harming others, one should try to stay away from these kinds of people this interaction will cause nothing but harm if dealing with someone looking for trouble and a troublesome situation. One should set a course for self-following one's own path trying ones best to stay away from harm as often as possible to remain ones peaceful state, and dealing with problems as the arrive trying never to cause problems for self or others while keeping ones safety in mind at all times while considering others safety.

(As humans we are all the same and capable of the same actions, there is no difference in life we live we live life and then we die leaving behind parts of self in life and memories of life and what once was living, one should try ones best to enjoy life as much as possible once ones necessities have been taking care of keeping one's life as save as possible with a positive outlook on life).

When one is ready **<u>learn to become more than one</u>** learning how to bled with opponents and life molding to ones surroundings when one learns how to, fill self with strength and power, and the control of one's strength and power focusing one what is and what isn't while one is searching for the best of one's self, maintaining constant control and balance and balance of self, staying strong in the mind and body strong as an elephant and as gentle as a floating butterfly constantly containing ones true power and strength unless needed. Maintain flexibility within and throughout while always training to maintain ones balance. Practice getting up after one falls starting over when one fails never giving up on self **(no one is perfect)** look at every action and technique in different lights and different direction to better the chance of finding ones answers to ones question while building the mind and body to fit ones functions in everyday life. **(Time + Practice + Progress) = <u>Greatness</u>**

One should stay in fight mode alert mode with total awareness when one's life is in danger, keeping one's eyes open and focused on the situation at hand and nothing else becoming one with ones surroundings to better protect one's self. Choose each path as if it where ones last path to choose, choosing with a clear mind controlling once action and state of mind as much as possible to increase the control of self-ready to defend one's self when one's life is threatened to better preserve one's life. Be aware of one's space and the space of one's attacker or attackers feeling the situation calculating the movements of self and attacker staying in one's untouchable state as much as possible taking action when one needs to always keeping ones range and the range of ones attacker in mind to better defend one's self, being able to set a path or paths to escape danger as much as humanly possible **(train one's mind and body to be able to find safety inside of combat and remain in one's untouchable state as much as possible until one has no need to defend ones self-ultimate goal).**

Another exercise great for total body fitness and total body awareness and coordination, soccer using the ball like a bean bag keeping ones eye on the ball at all times knowing where the ball is, how to control the ball at all times and learning how to predict where the ball will end up practices all kicks and kicking techniques to better learn self-becoming one with the ball and surroundings staying focused at all times just like playing with the bean bag, remembering to keep mental notes of all movements you never know what you will learn when one just plays around, staying focused and centered with in a relaxed state and relax state of mind, with the respect for life and life surroundings while having fun playing soccer.

It's easier to take opponents one at a time betting the chance of overcoming the altercation and handling the situation by canceling out ones opponent or opponents by canceling out closing the line or lines of danger and combination lining them up to knock them down. One shouldn't fight a battle one can't win unless one has no other choice in the matter. A warning should always be given when dealing with self-defense to warn attacker or attackers before acting in self-defense increasing the chance of remaining peaceful and staying in a peaceful state of mind, peace should be the answer in everyday life unless one is looking for trouble the opposite of self-defense, trouble free is the way to become. **Stay away from or try to stay away from harmful situations maintaining the peace and a peaceful state of mind.** One should never take kindness for weakness lessening the chance of underestimating ones opponent or opponents giving ones opponent the upper hand in combat, one should appreciate ones kindness and the kindness of others lessening the stress and strain of life. Words are just words even when they cut deep if words bother you then pretend that the words that bother you don't exist giving that word or those words no meaning, and with no meaning how can they bother you (**words are only words until words become action**).

Become space and maintain ones space to maintain ones foundation and one's balance, make ones space known controlling ones space, even a zero takes up space express your space and defend self when one's life is threatened or one's life put in jeopardy. Train oneself to extend ones points of contact by stretching keeping the body flexible to extend ones reach being able to connect from a further distance, search for one's true chi extending once ability to raise ones energy level with great control making one apart of the energy of life closing the loop of energy being a part of it, becoming part of energy, time, vibration, balance, and space its self and finally knowing one's self and always finding ways to better ones self. (**One can hold life in the palm of ones hands controlling what life brings to the life held, the question is what will one do with the life one hold**). <u>Great minds think alike or very similar</u>

To respect one's self is great, to respect ones teacher while one is being taut is great, but when one is ready, to respect one's self as ones teacher brings ones level of energy and understanding to a much higher level after learning enough to become ones teacher, this brings a different kind of understanding to self and others building ones confidence to a higher level with greater control never misusing ones power to harm only for protection staying humble within strength with a clear, calm, and relaxed mind and mental state, trying and training to never let ones anger and aggression become uncontrollable especially when one is mentally being pushed the wrong way only using self-defense to defend one's self, when ready eventually becoming a teacher of life, handing down ones knowledge to ones that truly deserves ones knowledge sharing ones energy and one's self-knowledge transferring ones energy of life and knowledge so one is really never forgotten, always keeping in mind that one must have control over ones great power ultimately becoming one with the world, time and space like the winds of time and the sunlight that brings life to so many, becoming one never limiting self in self-knowledge expanding self-becoming fluid knowing all direction of self and life becoming limitless, always learning to expands ones circle and circle of motion like a wave being pushed by water and air weighted down by gravity that holds everything like a mother and new born child, becoming fluid in action as well as theory always putting ones enemies or threats to self-outside of one's circle and circle of motion, staying untouchable when needed and becoming one with ones surrounding when possible, learning how to increase ones energy by adding energy from others, rather from knowledge learned from self or others or absorbing energy from one's life, learning what makes one happiest and how to maintain this state of happiest reaching ones state of peace and peace of mind. **(Play around with one's imagination this can help one escape life's stress and strain never getting lost inside ones imagination for too long knowing how to return to reality).**

Life becomes everything that life brings.

One can create an entire world within the realm of one's own personal space, learning one's self and ones range of motion. Learn to become space and part of ones surroundings, air can cause a house to move and tore apart like a hurricane, and as soft as a summer's breeze capable of cooling things down in the middle of the summer or helping to increase the intensity of fire blazing during a cool summer's night. **(Take life for what it is in the search for knowledge, loving life and what beauty it brings realizing the potential that life has).**

Better to walk away from a fight then to make an unwanted situation escalate into something that could possible take one's life.

Learn to move with one's sphere having no limitation to self-movements, no limitation.

In order to become what's wanted one must practice becoming what's wanted.

One shouldn't judge others until one has first and foremost judge one's self.

It's all in the way you look at things, usually one sees what one wants to see not always what is.

Never except some to act unlike themselves excepting them to act like themselves.

Power is what you make it and nothing more, as strong as an earthquake that shakes the world, sharing the world's vibration or bring life to the world by the suns light, always using wisdom when using ones power.

The truth will clear the mind of lies hidden within, clearing the conscience and freeing the mind of falseness, setting the truth free.

Knowledge is always useful to help one find the truth in one's life.

Life isn't fair especially in love and war, sometimes not getting what one wants. One can't really know another unless the other lets you understand their world.

One should learn one's body inside and out to better understand self and self-kind and to better understand life.

A friend of a friend is a friend unless ones friend's friend is ones enemy.

My enemy's enemy is a possible friend, unless that enemy's enemy is my enemy.

Sometimes it's better to listen and learn soaking up knowledge rather than to speak.

One must make the wisest of actions if one wants to succeed; staying focused and absorb what is and what isn't finding the truth.

Sometimes a friend can seem like an enemy when one's mind isn't clear, when it's one's mind that has become the enemy, cleans and clean the mind to make ones wisest decision learning what is and what isn't.

If one fails and makes the wrong decision usually one can correct ones problem and hopefully rewrite ones wrong and correct what was wrong.

In order to win sometime first one must lose in order to learn how to win.

Separate the real from the fake fact from fiction, and truly learn who is friend and who is foe.

Sometimes in the mist of battle one should step back and regroup ones thoughts in order to make the correct decision when one truly sees what is happening, the threat one see might not be a threat at all.

One shouldn't reveal ones truest inner most power unless needed; ones power should be controlled at all times while keeping a peaceful state and peaceful state of mind, unless one's life is in danger.

Learn self and peace of mind to learn what situation one should remain in maintaining safety and a peaceful peace of mind.

One should prepare for the future not being able to change the past unless one can change the past.

When problems occur in one's life, deal with one's problem, before ones problem escalates into a much bigger problem.

Actions speak louder than words sometime you have to show that you mean what you say and prove to self that one actually means what one says.

Balance self and work on living life doing what is safe and best for one's life and the lives of others. Defending one's self only when needed, doing **what's best for one's mind, body, heart, and one's spirit.**

Keep one's body free from <u>**unwanted**</u> bacteria, infections, toxins, waste, and any other unwanted pests and parasites.

One shouldn't lose love for self or others maintaining the peace with peaceful people and other creature that we share life with, trying to find the good in all.

One should always value loyalty, honest, dedication, respect, and honor.

One shouldn't blame someone else for ones actions, **(one shouldn't kill the messenger).**

Keep one's eyes and mind open, ones answer might ones answer in front of ones face, become opened minded helping one find the answers to one's question.

One shouldn't judge one too quickly one might make the wrong decision, and miss out of a great thing.

One mustn't let hatred get the best of self-making one make a wrong or unjust decision.

One shouldn't have to prove anything to anyone except for self when dealing with one's own life.

One shouldn't let obstacles get in ones way of making progress, there is an answer to one's question one just has to find the answers to ones questions.

Ones actions should always be true and true to self.

One shouldn't let hate seep into ones heart, never becoming hatred.

Take things for what they are and not pretend they are what you want them to be, separating what is from what isn't.

Live life in peace with a peaceful state of mind, balanced, and centered remembering that no one is perfect but one can reach one's own perfection as long as one continues to make progress while living one's life.

One shouldn't be greedy greed can quickly turn into hatred.

One should surround one's self with people and other things that one feels most comfortable being around.

Even in the greatest of times one should remain humble never taking life for granted remembering ones failures, and people lost in the struggle of life. What was gained can always be taken away learning from the good and bad experiences in life.

One should treat others like one treats self-building up as much good karma as possible to balance one's life.

One should practice being peaceful controlling ones power and learning one's self never limiting self while learning from life.

Time doesn't wait for life and living life takes time so one should take advantage of one's time.

(Find an idea + the <u>want</u> to succeed + the <u>action</u> it take to make the idea happen) = <u>Ones idea coming to life</u>

(Time + Dedication + Practice) = Skill
(Skill + Training + Time) = Experience
(Skill + Experience + Time) = Greatness
(Time + Hard work + Dedication) = Progress

One should have patience living life, sometimes water dries up just for the rain to fall again, learn the patterns and cycles of life to better learn self. Sometime staying steel or staying firm waiting for the answer to come like standing in a running river waiting for the water to flow downstream bringing what was up stream downstream feeding life to the river. Usually wiser to flow with the current of life then to wade up stream, and sometimes one must fight the stream like salmon fighting to produce life, unable to wait because time doesn't wait for life.

One should try never to take one's life though one might feel the burning urge blazing inside self, maintaining ones state of peace and a peaceful piece of mind living a peaceful existence.

Usually a great plan makes a great future if one puts ones plan into action continuing making progress in one's plan. (**Practice makes ones perfection**).

In order to find one's self one must be truly honest with one's self, if not one will find someone other than self.

If one falls down, one can usually climb back up finding the ladder of success again focusing one ones goals and learning for one's life experiences.

Sometimes it's better to forgive the wrongs done and walk away than to enter chaos, keeping ones peace and peace of mind is usually the answer to a stressful situation staying relaxed stopping back from the problem to better understand the problem at hand to better solve ones problem or problems.

Even the strongest man or woman will or can feel small and weak when all the odds are against them, this is the best time for one to find a different kind of strength, the strength within ones inner strength training the mind to handle stressful and unkind situations building the mind as well as the body.

Better to surround one's self with peaceful people to maintain ones level of peace and doing what is best to maintain this peace.

Sometimes in bad times one must lay in the pit in order to learn how to pick one's self up never giving up hope for success, always trying to maintaining a positive outlook of life even when life seems grim.

One shouldn't burn a bridge that one might have to cross later on in life always trying to make the right decisions, planning for success never failure.

One shouldn't start problems, it's always best to live in peace together with peaceful people and peaceful things to better the chance of a longer existence.

Skill, knowledge, and life's experiences and self-knowledge will help one find one's self, and one will better understand one's self and others.

Learn to live life and the protection of one's life, living in peace defending self only when needed while ones learns to love life again in a new light with a different knowledge of self.

One shouldn't ask someone else to do something they wouldn't do.

One must train to be self sufficient

Trust must be earned the respected for trust is something that has to be proven to self and others building the trust within ones relationships in one's life, building good karma within one's life. (**Practice makes perfect no one is perfect but one can reach one's own perfection**).

Special thanks to all the martial artist and fighters of the world, Shaolin, Wu Tang, and every other clan or sect in the martial arts world, and to my parents and family. I will forever love and respect, and let all the worlds sleeping soldier's lye.

Peace never chaos

- Ones goal is to create peace out of or unwanted situation, to be able to walk away from an altercation with one's life, a great martial artist can do this without any action at all, and one must learn how to control a situation to deflate ones problem or threat.
- Respect plays a great role in self-defense and life, sometimes it only take a sprinkle of water to extinguish the flame, but one spark can ignite the world itself, there must be control within ones actions and movements, control is the key, without control one may cause injury to self or others, one must train to control self to become capable to control others, control power is the key.
- One can reach a target at a greater distance if one increases ones range, by using the outer realm out ones circle to increase distance in action within action.
- I have been trying to become better the self by changing ideas and actions and my frame of thought, but the outcome is always the same, no matter how much progress I achieve, or experience I learn I still remain the same person, I still remain me, one should learn to love one's self no matter what the outcome to remain whole. Refrain from becoming partial, remain whole, remain one.
- One must use all of the scenes and surrounding to locate ones opponent and/or object to better feel ones environment, knowing yourself and ones surrounding can often help in gaining leverage within action, a side step to change the lines or points of attack to help one find balance and leverage in action to increase the possibility of success within action, and one must follow through when and only when ones heart is in it. Protection of self is key in self-defense, one must respect life, because life can turn to death in an instant.
- One must become like the mongoose who hunts the snake that lies between the weeds, staying cautious, mobile and alert in action to defeat action.
- Never give up, one must become better - better then self.
- One must never get in the way of one's self progress
- One must bow to show respect because life is precious

- Imagine a circle of range around self, and opponent to better ones ability of action, one should react when needed to better conserve one's energy.
- One should be able to express one's inner peace externally
- One should feel comfortable within the space that surrounds self, and the space that surround ones opponent, to better control the outcome of one's situation, one should remain calm and relax, and move without mind and body, and act as if one is watching a battle from the outside realm, seeing all and missing nothing, this will give one the ability to act without thought and will as one becomes life in its truest form and state, bending the world at will.
- Train the eye and body to see what is present and what will come, body language tells all.
- The art of combat is to survive at all cost, there are no winners in battle, one must find true peace within chaos, and one must protect one's self at all time, and only act when needed.
- One is self and everything that surrounds self, one can become anything that one wishes to be, molding self in one's own image cutting away the nothingness of life, and leaving the image of one's own life, creating something out of nothing, this is obtained with great patience, time and knowledge of self and what surrounds self.
- Not everyone likes to become the same, because no one is the same one must find self within the most of life
- It is always best to hold or keep a strong mind, keeping the falsehood of life from within, again one must separate fact from fiction to maintain mental health and stability no matter what the situation may be.
- Wise men say you can tell the identity and history of a lion by the cuts and scars that line the ear, this is also true in self, one's imperfection tell the tale of one's life, one should live without regret, because one's history tell it all.
- Fear is a part of life but one shouldn't let fear or fear or death cloud the mind, it is best to concentrate on what is living, because life takes life more often the death, life is precious and full of pain and must be protected until the end. Death is not the hunter of life, life is, but one should never rush the end of life because death is certain for all life

- It is always better to stand for something, than to fall for anything one should never let doubt fill the mind, one only has to find the answer to one's problem, to solve one's problems, once one finds the answer one only has to apply ones answer to life.
- Love and hate can penetrate the thickest of hearts, one should be aware of what lies within, the energy within can change what surrounds self.
- It is best to always keep the mind and spirit free like an open window revealing new opinion as life moves on, setting no limits, no boundaries upon self, it is imagination that set one free, imagination is the fruit of life making anything possible, set no limits upon self and one can do and become the impossible
- Never let the outside world blind your judgment within the stress and strain of??? can bring even the strongest man to his knees, one must endure and overcome the many obstacles of life, while maintaining cool and clear state of mind eliminating every obstacle that stands in the way of progress, even if that obstacle standing in the way is self, one must overcome ones obstacle in order to gain progress, there should be no limits in life, no boundaries. One should clear a path in which one has no obstacles standing in the way creating a clear vision of ones goals and dreams.
- There is always a way or solution to solve every problem or situation, one only to find the correct way or direction to find the way or answer.
- A straight line isn't always the answer, sometimes it's best to Manu??? Around, over or under an obstacle to reach one's target or goal, progress is the k??? And one of the first step in obtaining one's goals and dreams. One must never give up, one must become better

(progress + time + skill + experience) = <u>Road to Greatness</u>

| Greatness - the object of be??? Greater than self. |

- Nothing worth having rarely comes easy, time can tell the tale of a great man all you have to do is look at where he has been. The past tells the future. A wise man once said, it is always best to make the best out of every precious moment, life is short and bittersweet that is why it is best to never give up.

- Sometime one only has to look back to realize where one has been???Forward, and how far one or has wishes to travel. Never give up on self because self??? All one really has to hold on to.

*. One should use the arms and legs like a tigers uses his whiskers, giving one a six sense of awareness, using one arm directed behind to prepare for any sudden attacks. This will also help one counter attack before or after an opponent's attack. The whole body can be used in this way to better protect self from one's opponent or opponents.

- Awareness is the key to protection, without awareness one will be left open for attack. Become one with self, one's opponent and the elements or one's surroundings to better protect self.

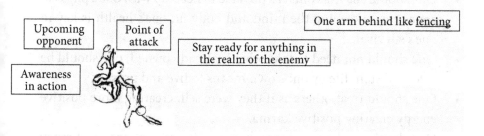

Upcoming opponent

Point of attack

One arm behind like fencing

Stay ready for anything in the realm of the enemy

Awareness in action

- Practicing phantom techniques [mental techniques without real physical action mental sparing]. This technique will increase your ability of awareness by reprogramming the mind and body to act without thought, this technique takes a lot of training, but if done right this technique can increase ones skill 100 fold.

- Life will get hard, and then harder, leaving one callused and hard, better skilled with greater experienced. Leaving one with a better way of living life, as long as one can cope with the stress and strain of life, one must be able to adapt to even the hardest situation, and survive, there is always a way out of a troublesome situation, one only has to look in the right direction to find the right path. [Life is always the most important priority.]

- It is better for one to say nothing, then for one to speak much about nothing.

- One should never take life for granted, life is precious and should never be overlooked, because without life there is only death.

- It is best to clean the body at least once a day, ridding the body of toxins, dirt, and oils that suffocate the body, clogging the skin and pores, bathing brings health, vitality and a new outlook on life, and brings forth clean and positive energy after every after the body has been cleaned, out with the old energy and in with new positive energy. Keeping the mind, body, and spirit free from contamination. Daily bathing also helps in clearing and cleaning the sinuses giving one greater power in action and mobility. Apply vitamins and moisturizers to the body to aid the skin rid itself from infection sickness, and disease, this should be done daily for the best results, giving the body a great healthy glow, energizing the body making one feel better, free, and clean.
- One should shave as often as possible to keep up with one's physical appearance, keeping the mind and body fit, one's health is key to one's survival.
- One should not need to take what is already owned, one should be able to sustain life by one's own means to live and prosper.
- One should treat others as if they were self, creating more positive energy creating positive karma.
- One should not borrow more than one can return, one must repay all debt to keep the peace, this creates positive energy or positive karma, helping one to create and build strong bonds that will become helpful in ones future.
- Borrowing from someone without repaying creates and builds unwanted tension and negative energy or negative karma, leaving one's life tainted with potential problems and stress in life, it is always best to repay what is owed leaving one's mind free from regret.
- One should never expect someone who does a wrong to regret. This is why it is always best to surround one's self with positive energy and/or karma to lessen the chance of negative energy scrapping in to cloud one's mind body and spirit.
- [A wise man once told me it is better to learn something, then to learn nothing at all.] One should fill the mind with knowledge instead of the nothingness of life.

- One should never point the finger at the innocent, it is always best to point the finger in the direction of the one responsible, <u>one must separate fact from fiction</u>. This is the way to a strong mind.
- When one becomes surrounded by grief and despair at the crossroads of life left without direction, it is best to continue forward until one finds ones path.
- It is never too late to fix a problem, (life is progress)

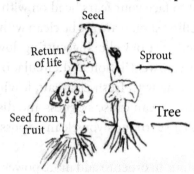

- Life starts from the seed which sprouts and turns into the tree which produces fruit and returns the seed [or returns life] to life. One must take great care of ones seed in order to ensure a great and health life so one can watch his seed grow. <u>Life is most precious</u> and number one priority.
- One must never lie to self-one must search for the truth and what is true.
- By thinking and speaking the truth one can create the ability of insight to the past, present, future, by thinking and speaking the truth one begins to see what is true, life is life and life will be life until death, life and death always stays the same, there is always a pattern or set of the same, (common ground) things needed for life to survive before the end, if you can recognize the pattern you can reveal the next move within the pattern but one must be cautious a pattern can change pattern within a blink of an eye so if one wishes to see the next move, one only has to watch. By thinking and speaking the truth one becomes something <u>true</u>, this is best on the light side of the realm, with positive energy, light karma. One must

be patient while calm and collective when practicing this skill. [The truth can become ones greatest enemy if one is not careful]

The mind is very strong make sure what you think is true, actually is true.

- It is not in ones best interest to turn your back on the ones that mean you harm it is best to face your fears head on with both eyes open.
- Ones home or dwelling should always be clean with a pleasant smell, giving one an better sense of wellbeing, cutting down the possibility of sickness and disease ventilation and circulation of air will also help, filling your home with fresh clean air, leaving your dwelling smelling clean, stale air can cause sickness and disease, it is best to keep everything that surrounds you clean as possible to better the health of life.
- The hip has two joints, in order to add more power to every kick one only has to follow through, using the hip as a <u>spring</u>, once you cock back use the hip joint to add extra power/strength to every kick, one must keep complete balance through the complete movement, and this will increase the energy of movement. This is true with other limbs as well.
- The joints are involved in almost every movement the body makes, to increase ones energy in motion start from the farthest joint to the tip of the limb used. When you feel the ball of the bringing the energy through joint in motion, then you are moving correctly, one must take note of ones movements in action in order to move correctly during or within action to make the most of ones' actions.
- It is always better for one to prepared, then for one to be without, preparation is everything when one's life and wellbeing is at stake. It is best for the honey to have pollen collected so that the honey bee does not run out of honey to eat.
- One should collect the necessities of life so one is always prepared for life, one should stay prepare for??? Chaos with greater??? greater passion, for life is everything and without one's life there is only peace, survival is always ones number one priority it is best to

prepare for every situation one may encounter to better protect one's life.

- It is possible to intercept an action or <u>counter</u> an action by timing ones opponent's actions opening up a target, then acting when ones opponent's window of defense has been opened leaving then open for attack or action. Find the pattern of your opponent's actions and one's opponent becomes like an open book that has already been read, making ones attack or counter attack action and counter action more successful.

- It is better to have a wide range of techniques to limit the probability of predictability. It is better to be unpredictable having no pattern, but remaining fluid and mobile in action keeping ones opponent guessing instead of knowing ones next move. Find ways to complete an action, attack, or counter attacks from different angles to complete the same function furthering ones unpredictability, a straight line is the quickest way from point <u>A</u> to point <u>B</u> but one might have to maneuver around, over, or under an obstacle to reach ones target an order to make ones action successful, one must stay <u>strong</u>, <u>flexible</u> and <u>agile</u> to achieve this <u>ability</u>. If ones actions aren't successful, then ones actions will fail, one must practice technique in motion to learn how to use ones technique in action. A failed action is of no use no matter how strong it may be, one must use timing experience, and skill to ensure the success of ones actions, or counter actions. One must ensure the success of technique in order to succeed. As long as one makes progress, one is taking the correct steps to find success.

- <u>Timing</u> will give one the <u>ability</u> to <u>increase</u> the amount of power, and energy to ones technique in the time provided by ones opponent, pay attention to all opportunities while keeping a cool, and calm mental state remaining patient before and after the moment of attack or/ and action, releasing the correct amount of energy to complete ones action and/or technique.

- <u>Leverage</u> is the key to winning all battles. One only has to apply pressure and one's opponent will crumble, but one must never underestimate ones opponent life is full of surprises.

- Those who live life with struggle and pain become stronger than those who live life without the stress of life.
- Any successful technique is a technique worth using, one should find more uses for the same technique. A strike or blow can also be used as a block or an opening for a counter attack. There are more than one use for every technique or skill, experience will show you the way.
- An untrained child??? As dangerous as a man??? Holding a semi-automatic weapon capable of anything. One must train all children and students proper pointing each one toward a just and righteous path, wrong teachings can also become a great treat to life, one should always search for what is real, true, and just to limit or eliminate the possibility of treat.
- When one side of the body takes motion, the opposite side takes motion as well, to balance the whole, when one moves, one should move as one to create greater energy, power, and balance in motion. The right side has to move with the left, ones upward motion must move with the downward motion in order for the whole to take motion. One should remain whole like a sealed example to counteract ones opposite side, when the body remains still sometimes it's hard to notice the opposite side movement, but if one pays close attention to one's body, one will take notice of ones actions in motion, become aware of one's own movements. Walking is also a great way to prove this theory. It is best to prove life to be true.
- Throwing a strike or blow with either arms or legs should be thrown and/or conducted as like a spring for added power to technique follow through the full and complete action pushing the force or energy through and throughout ones target for best result. Control is always a key factor for safety purposes. The sling-shot effect is also a great way to eject or pass ones power and/or ones energy building up the necessary muscles to complete ones action, then releasing ones energy when the amount of power has been achieved as the pebble which represents ones energy is released.

The force of one's strike and/or blow will increase the amount of energy or/and power to ones technique by added energy or/and power to one's technique. Control of action is vital to protect one's life and limbs, be aware of the amount of pressure one's body can handle to lessen the chance of injury when dealing with energy and/or power use caution when dealing with energy and power to lessen injury

- Spring concentrated energy another example is the Hercules shrimp now which is able to break through harder shells of other sea creatures under water, they can generate almost the same amount of energy or power as a nine millimeter gun from underwater with this spring action technique.
- Failure will teach one how to loose, and success and experience how to win, but one also can find success in failure if one learns from ones mistakes. <u>Knowledge</u> of <u>self</u> and <u>life</u>, and <u>success</u> in <u>life</u> is the <u>key to success.</u>
- One should practice stopping ones opponent's action before ones opponents action becomes vital, usually at the middle joint of each limb, at the shoulder, elbow, hips, and knees, stopping the action before the snap, preventing one's opponent from reaching their full potential in attack.

Restrict the ability of action by catching the action before its completed, counter action is possible then, smother ones opponent with force to restrict ones opponents force or energy, stopping all action. Opening up ones opponent for action.

Note to self-absorbing ones energy and/or power from ones opponent

One should not look at self-defense as an object of destruction but as a chance to create a peaceful situation out of chaos, one should find a ways to make peace out of chaos, as long as peace is possible, one's peace and control of power should become greater than the possible of destruction, the objective is to defeat the possibility of destruction to self and others, but one should always keep self as one's number one priority,

- Learn to become protection, and learn to protect want is most valuable to self.
- Even in times of peace and plenty, one should never trust thy enemy.
- Any technique that successful is a great technique.
- Any technique that works becomes the cure, solution, or answer to one's problems. (Whatever works becomes the best solution) (Anything that works).
- Adaptation is key to life. One must be able to change like the wind.
- One must learn to face ones fear, in order to live a peaceful existence, fear can cause one to panic and make the wrong decision which increases the cause of failure, (control one fear and become fearless.)
- Repetition will reprogram the mind and body to act without thought, without mind (practice and repetition is everything.)
- It is always best to be honest loyal, and just, (except in times of war.) The only purpose of war is to win, there is no other option. Its best to act wisely planning every move like the game of chess to increase the probability of success.
- Like the samurai, it is better to die free, then to live life as a slave, this is why self-defense is most vital to life, because one's life is the most important object in one's life, protect it to the end with all ones might, especially in times of war.
- One must always know what one is capable of, to better see the outcome of success, and to better increase the possibility of success.
- Know thy self like one should know thy enemy.
- War is a battle between differences of options that's all and that's it, and leverage is the key to success.
- The battle between self and one's opponent is the same as the battle within that's why it is best to understand self, one's opponent and

what one is fighting for (love thy self, and understand thy enemy). One should never love thy enemy, for thy enemy will show no mercy in the heat of battle and/or combat

Inspired By Greatness
So much to learn so little time
By: <u>Kevin Green</u>

- Trained weapons <u>should</u> only be use in practice or protection
- Once you enter the realm of an opponent, you must train to be able to mold to your opponent and take your opponents actions to benefit self, counters are very helpful when trying to turn an opponent, actions against them.
- <u>Train</u> for <u>agility</u>, <u>speed</u>, <u>focus</u>, and <u>power</u> one must be able to maintain composure at all time. Power must be control by a professional. During combat eye open, mind focus.
- <u>Train</u> to win (<u>time</u> + <u>practice</u>) = <u>greatness</u>
- Nothing is perfect, but train for perfection.
- Maintain the inner beast when anger is at its greatest to overcome self, to win, or overcome opponent, or to overcome self, control the inner beast before its controls. No one's perfect.
- <u>Balance</u> <u>training</u> standing on a leg for <u>10 mines</u> + each leg.
- Practice stance transfer during techniques
- <u>Body manipulation</u> usually by locking a limb or catching an opponent off balance, is very useful in a match throwing an opponent off balance.
- Sometimes you have to lose before you can win sometimes helps to gain experience.
- Explain more about <u>energy</u> <u>transfer</u> <u>theory</u>. [[Insert picture 012 here]] <u>don't stop</u> at the end of act let the energy follow thru???

> No picture 012 on Supplied Images
> image placement is on the bullet list

<u>Train</u> to able to use your environment to your advantage. Almost anything you can be used to help preserve life.

- To be able to win most of the time you have to know when to take advantage of the opponent or opponent's during combat.
- Sparing can and will help in this training. Learn how to mold an overcome your opponent from inside they're circle. Every moment is done differently every time molding to each situation.
- Sometime you have to get out of the <u>line of danger</u> if you are unable to block, than dodge.
- When <u>throwing</u> a punch or kick make sure the blow in centered and make sure you follow through and snap after the target (whip like action).
- While <u>training</u> with an <u>open eye</u> try to stay <u>out</u> of the *<u>line of danger</u>, very important especially when trying to be untouchable, when an opponent's realm.
- Sometime you just have to wait until your opponent gives you an opportunity and you must take advantage of that moment. Time plays a great factor??? Deciding the victor in close range him???

Maintaining your <u>untouchable state</u> is very <u>helpful</u> when needing to catching your breath. Catch opponent off balance and make a vital blow before your opponent make a vital blow. Once engaged in combat try to finish the battle as soon as possible to reduce the amount of damage done to self. Usually the quickest action wins, unless the action has been beaten by power or another act.

<u>Line closing</u> doesn't matter how you close the line of danger as long as the line is closed to open up a weak spot or <u>open</u> location in opponent fighting or/and combat stance.

Opponent off balance
<u>Blocking</u> in line closing
When you fall down and get back up and stay up.

- Keep eye on <u>opponent</u> or/and <u>opponents</u> remember where their <u>circles</u> range of motion are at all times <u>when</u> possible.

Closest target

Sometimes you need to, <u>speed</u> <u>up</u> in order to beat an opponent to attack or sometimes slowdown in order to meet target at the correct time. Can't hit an opponent unless opponent is in??? Depending on weapon used.

<u>Train</u>: to be able to move <u>in</u> and <u>out</u> the opponents <u>range</u> <u>of</u> <u>sight</u> usually if they can't see they won't win unless they have the ability to locate you when in the blind spot, train ears to locate opponent when there are in the blind spot, try to plan their next move.

- If opponent or opponents beat you to the <u>punch</u> or <u>kick</u>, try to push their energy + plus your energy added, and send it back towards them as quick as possible, or/counter if there is time; pushing an opponent off balance can be the deciding factor in a sparring match.
- When in the realm of an opponent, something <u>closer</u> is better using the shortest tools to transfer energy. Throwing off an <u>unwanted</u> attack with a counter or block at the correct time, opening up a point of entry. Once the door is open don't close it until the match is over if not the opponent might have time to block/parry or/and attack unless they are blocked or countered or put now.
- One should stay out of the <u>line of danger</u> waiting for an opening presents, itself, and once it does to advantage of every open moment if you're capable to do so, as soon as possible in order to win, one shouldn't hesitate when in combat. <u>Focus</u> on the <u>target</u> at hand and <u>complete</u> the action while the <u>time</u> is available
- <u>Each</u> <u>action</u> must be true to self and must blend in and/or with opponent or opponents. Until combat is finished. Stay focus at all time, controlling anger + aggression while focusing ones energy doesn't matter if it's hand to hand combat and/or actions with weapons, one must become one with self and surroundings. <u>Balance</u> is key
- Try to practice moving from one target to another without mind with complete focus controlling self. Discipline

- Be careful when in <u>fight mood</u> one can get lost stuck in an uncomfortable state, this state hits a lot of strain on the mind and body, so keep mind focused and clean. <u>Control</u> anger and <u>aggression</u> as much as possible and focus it in the correct direction, way, or/ and fashion.
- One must respect self, and <u>pain</u> of self???
- Pain shouldn't stop you unless the pain become???
- <u>Sometimes</u> the answer you find lies in the past and sometimes the past is the future.
- Another great <u>agility</u> <u>workout</u> and/or <u>exercise</u> great for leg and foot coordination and all around body coordination is playing hacky sack a small sac fitted with either beans, sand or even pebbles, try keeping it in the air, kicking like a (ball, soccer) or try catching it with feet, legs, arms, or/and the rest of the body, use knees also while playing, working and exercises always feel better when having fun just play around.

Just play around with the hacky sack.

- In order to learn your body, you must first learn how to use your body, to learn to use one's body, one must learn one range of motion limb limit, body limits. Learn your flower.
- Drinking hot liquids help to loosen the mucus in the nasal pathway, steam helps also breathing in stream (caution) make sure the liquids, or steam doesn't burn. (Check the temperature and make sure it's <u>safe</u>) <u>Steam</u> is also a great way to help clean pores helps to release toxins through sweat * Find a way to??? the skin for training with hard surfaces, rep's and more <u>reps</u>. <u>Mind</u> <u>over</u> <u>matter</u>, there is <u>no pain</u> *Any progress, is <u>great</u> progress no matter what life bring make <u>progress</u> and if you ran into problems ask, don't let pride or ego get in the way of <u>self-progress</u>. No <u>one's</u> perfect, but one can reach one own <u>perfection</u> with practice, * <u>practice</u> makes perfect or close to it.
- Sometimes you have to let go of things to hold a grip on something else. Be true to self, it's very easy to lose one's self in fantasy, if one is not <u>true</u> <u>to</u> <u>self</u>.

- Must find balance in order to complete function. Balance through the whole action not partial.
- (Usually hoping for the best, expecting the worst) Energy, wave produced by the body's ability to transfer energy, directly outward.
- One must remember that to respect one's self and very important respect your opponent and never underestimate self or opponent, self-defense is for self-defense only unless, in a match with opponent or opponents. Respect life and keep in mind that know/no one can have total power, energy must be spread out to all. Remain cool, calm, and collective, and relax.

- Everything in life has a beat, find the beat, feel it, and become one with the beat. Molding to life and when life brings, step by step.

Range of motion

- Must show respect for great energy and respect the ones who left this great way of expression, one self and remember that skill and one's life may end at any time, take advantage of one's time and do what is good for self and have fun. But be safe at all times.
- Give opponent no time to make action, no space, close their circle with great speed accuracy and power with the correct timing, locking limbs will help with this type of training. Be careful when locking joints this make breaking bones very easy, be careful not to harm sparring partner, try not to harm. Self Defense is all about protecting one's self.

Joint locking and breaking

Press down on the joint find leverage and press up on the end of limb until you press down feel the press of the bone give way. Be care not to harm only protect this form is very dangerous and painful for the person with the broken limb.

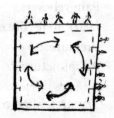

- Broken

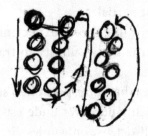

- Place bone back in place

- Add splints in front back and sides wrapped up not to tight

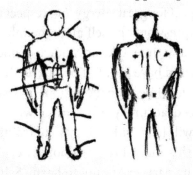

- Until break in fix fused back together.
- Learn how to fix the <u>break</u>.
- Pain relievers.
- Learn to fix breaks and other medical techniques
- Pressure???
- Acupuncture???

- Try stretching to help find balance and throughout technique. <u>Focus</u> on the position of body and each limb, know your <u>flower</u> and <u>circle</u> and/or <u>personal</u> <u>space</u>.

- Always keep <u>hands</u>, and feet ready to block, or attack (body also, (whole body). <u>Protect</u> head and face and <u>eyes to maintain</u> <u>visual</u> contact with target and/or opponent. <u>Harding</u> to <u>maintain</u> an <u>action</u>, when <u>one loses</u> the <u>ability</u> to see or any other senses. Protect self, self-kind at all times if possible. (<u>Self Defense</u>)
- <u>Protect</u> <u>vital</u> areas of the body. Learn self so one will be able to make a split second <u>decision</u> when it really counts. Be careful when entering the ring, whether inside the ring or outside the ring maintain one's self (self-composure.)
- <u>Meditation</u> is very helpful when trying to find <u>inner peace</u> and <u>peace of mind</u>. There is also <u>another</u> <u>world</u> <u>within</u> <u>world</u> when you meditate, you can either clean your mind and think of nothing or take a trip outside of one's self. This takes much training and? Practice this type of train especially when stressed or depressed find one self and want makes one happy.

(Imagination holds the key)

- One should <u>train</u> to <u>cut</u> <u>through</u> the <u>air</u>, and <u>space</u> to <u>reach</u> <u>target</u> with <u>great speed.</u>
- <u>Speed</u> drills will help with this, start of <u>slow</u>, and with <u>practice</u> <u>build</u> up <u>speed</u>, make sure that you <u>add</u> <u>power</u>, and <u>accuracy</u> to your training. Then focus on <u>controlling</u> this <u>power</u> to better find self. Their areas cut through air and space faster than a wider <u>surface</u> world. To reach ones with greater speed and accuracy to make contact with <u>wanted</u> targets, very important. A beat will help in this, <u>different</u> <u>rhythm</u> to <u>different</u> <u>beats</u>, and sometimes even <u>off</u> <u>beat</u> to fit the <u>situation</u> at <u>hand</u> and depending on opponent and/or targets. Place a target punching pad, punching bag kicking pad, etc. Something to practice on without hurting. <u>Repetition</u>, with <u>correct</u> <u>form</u> of <u>self,</u> balance keeping up with the pace given, when ready change rhythm and change and build up speed. (One must practice to become better than one was.)

<u>Flatter</u> <u>surface</u> moves quicker than the air, space and maybe T???

- In order to live in <u>peace</u>, one must <u>live</u> <u>in</u> <u>a</u> <u>peace</u> state <u>of</u> <u>mind</u>. Hoping that the little energy <u>rubs</u> off and/or flows to another. In order to be peaceful <u>usually</u> you must live in <u>peace</u>. No bodies perfect, but one can reach that own <u>perfection</u>. More important for one to <u>maintain</u> their <u>space</u> and keep their <u>space</u> <u>safe</u>. Find the beat to one's own path. Keeping others in <u>consideration</u>. We are all the same. We are <u>life</u>. There is no difference in life. We are born we live, and then we pass on. Enjoy life as much as possible while keeping <u>safety</u> in mind. Where does [[insert picture 028 here]] the energy go? I wonder her do you track the flow of energy? Maybe it something different. Maybe it's just the <u>food</u> <u>chain</u>. Or maybe it's something else.

> No picture 028 on Supplied Images
> image placement is on the bullet list

- Stay relaxed and focused and remember it is <u>always</u> <u>easier</u> to take on an opponent situation, and/or obstacle <u>one at</u> a <u>time</u> for a better chance of <u>success</u>, cancel out opponents and/or obstacles by blocking the line of action and/or attack. Line them up and then take them down.

Situation life threatened (close line of danger)

- One shouldn't fight a battle one can't win unless there is no other option self-defense. A <u>warming</u> should always be advised when it alert or attack or fight mood to better the chance of peace. <u>Peace</u> <u>should</u> always be the answer in everyday life unless one is looking for trouble. Trouble free is the way to become. Stay away from or try ones best to stay away from harmful situation keeping the peace.
- Very important one shouldn't take kindness for weakness??? One should appreciate kind people and kindness lessens the level of <u>stress</u> and <u>strain</u>.
- Don't let words cut to deep words are only words until they become something else.
- <u>Another</u> <u>agility</u> <u>exercises</u>. Great for <u>body awareness</u> keep <u>eyes,</u> <u>ears</u>, and <u>sense</u> of <u>touch</u> and <u>awareness</u> <u>focused</u> on the <u>ball</u> or ano<u>ther</u> <u>objected</u> used. <u>Became</u> of ones <u>surroundings</u> with practicing this exercise.

- Stay <u>balanced</u> and <u>focus</u> on hitting the ball with control. Like <u>soccer</u> or (<u>football</u>) <u>Great</u> <u>leg</u> and <u>body</u> <u>workout</u>. (Like hacky sack play) (Open minded possibilities)

- One can <u>practice</u> <u>technique</u>, <u>playing</u> with a ball. Just have fun, and keep track of the movements made and practice. You never know what you will learn! Stay <u>balanced</u> and <u>centered</u>, <u>calm</u> and <u>relaxed</u> with a <u>peaceful</u> <u>peace</u> <u>of</u> <u>mind</u>, with the <u>respect</u> for life and life surroundings.

<u>Become</u> <u>Space</u> and <u>Live</u> <u>Life</u>, with <u>Much</u> <u>Respect</u> <u>Honor</u> and Loyalty searching to become one's best.

- <u>One can create an entire world within ones person space. Learn ones range of motion.</u> Become <u>space</u> and what surrounds it. Air can cause a house to move. If one is in a house is one apart of the house. And if something happens to the house, can one be harmed? These are the <u>questions</u> one must ask one's self when living day to day.
- <u>Become space</u>, even a zero takes up space. Maintain <u>flexibility</u> at all times or when possible.
- <u>To close</u> the gap and <u>extend</u> points and <u>connect</u> the <u>chain</u> to <u>reach</u> an <u>everlasting</u> <u>source</u> of <u>energy</u>, no matter the <u>kind</u> of <u>energy</u>
- <u>Closing</u> the <u>loop</u> of <u>energy</u>, <u>time</u> <u>vibration</u>, and <u>space</u> <u>seek</u> <u>balance</u>.
- <u>Positive and Negative</u> space knowledge to help extend <u>life</u>. Safely (Take <u>life</u> for whatever it takes)

(What is or what isn't (life))

Knowledge and the search for it after needs are met, and living life,

(One can hold <u>life</u> in the <u>palm</u> of the <u>hand</u> and <u>not</u> <u>realize</u> its potential)

- Remain on <u>relaxed</u> <u>state</u>, <u>one</u> <u>must</u> <u>train</u> to be relax, <u>relaxed</u> <u>thinking</u> cool, <u>calm</u>, and <u>collective</u>. Relaxed. Remain calm. <u>One</u> thinks clearer when in a relaxed (<u>state</u> <u>of</u> <u>mind</u>). One side soft one side hard

(Starting with a high #'s of reps the decrease the amount of rep making easier to complete more reps)

(Action theory) (Theory action)

Become whole self-become real
Find your center

<u>No limits</u> expand self-become fluid, become space, and become one

<u>All</u> <u>direction</u> limitless
Become space

- Learn to expand ones circle of motion <u>like</u> a <u>wave</u> <u>in</u> <u>water</u>, become fluid in action and theory. Put opponent outside of circle and/or range of motion. Stay <u>untouchable</u> as long as possible. <u>Using</u> one's own energy plus opponent's energy to do so.
- Play around with one's imagination, to better find self.

Life is too short

- Very important one must train to become, and remain happy, so one can reach ones happiest and remain happy.
- To <u>respect</u> <u>one's</u> <u>self</u> is great. To <u>respect</u> ones <u>teacher</u> and/or <u>training</u> is great, but to respect <u>one's</u> self as teacher and/or trainer brings one's self to a <u>higher</u> or more <u>in depth</u> feeling about one's self, (when ready) confidence is key when training one's self or being trained by a teacher and/or trainer. When one is ready. Stay <u>humble</u>, with a clear, and calm mind, when training. Don't let <u>anger</u> and <u>aggression</u> push you the wrong way.
- Self-control as much as humanly possible.

- I hurt someone I love, and it's up to that person to forgive or not. I must live with what I have done, hoping for forgiveness. <u>One</u> must learn <u>self-control</u>. So this doesn't happen again.
- One must choose their own path wisely, so, one will have no or less regrets.
- To know one's self, one must learn one's self, learn oneself when partial, and when whole

<u>Theory</u>   <u>Action</u>

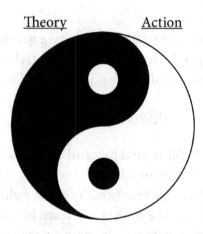

Together makes one whole

*• Become <u>space</u>, while maintaining one's own space. Mold to environment. Become space become air, become fluid, and become <u>one</u>.

<u>Balance</u>

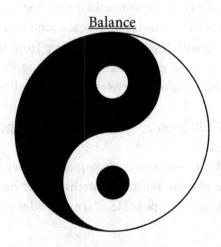

- Learn to be more than one when ready, than learn to become than so on. When one is ready.
- Feel one's power and learn focus, learn self.
- Maintain content balance. Stay centered (form foundation).
- Strong as an elephant, gentle as a butterfly

One must control self as much as one can, when dealing with power and great energy

- Maintain flexibility throughout. Maintain balance
- <u>Start over again</u> and learn each idea and/or technique from a totally different outlook. Build body's muscles to fit function better.

Progress = Greatness

- Better to be peaceful around peaceful creatures to maintain peace.
- People and other creatures do what they have to want to it's always best to do the correct action (what's correct right)
- Sometimes one must lie in the pit to learn how to pick one self-up. One must not give up hope. Maintain a positive outlook on life.
- One shouldn't burn a bridge that may be needed to be crossed later on in one's life. Better to plan then plan some more, nothing in life is promised except death.
- One shouldn't start problems especially when problems aren't needed. It is always best to live in peace together with peaceful people and other creatures. With peace, one will be able to live a <u>longer existence</u> with <u>less problems to keep from starting wars</u>.
- Skill, knowledge and experience and self-knowledge will help in finding one's self, once one learns one self, one will better understand others
- Life is life is life!!! <u>Protection for life living for peace</u>, <u>self-defense only</u> when needed.
- One shouldn't ask someone to do something they wouldn't do.
- Trust must be earned, trust is something that has to be practiced every day or as often as possible. Karma good = peace and peace of mind.

- Even the strongest man will feel small <u>when all the odds are against them</u>. This is the best time to find different strength inner internal strength. One must <u>mentally train</u> for this <u>internal power</u>.

*(When possible create More Life Laws)

(Better full than empty)

- One should never take another's one's life even though one might be able to one should live a <u>peaceful</u> <u>existence</u>.
- The cup is <u>half full</u>. (See the <u>truth</u> not empty, try)
- A good <u>plan</u> usually makes a better or/and <u>great</u> future. (Practice makes perfect)
- In order to find yourself, one must be truly honest with oneself, if not you will find something or/and someone else. Usually the truth will set you free.
- No matter what situation life offers, one can usually climb back to the top again using the knowledge one has gained from life experiences, as long as one has the ability to see down the path focusing on the goal and/or next step to completing an action.
- Sometimes it's better to forgive and walk away than to enter excepting chaos, peace and a peaceful peace of mind usually is the

answer to stressful situation relaxing and stepping back from the problem to better focus on the problem.

- One shouldn't reveal one truest inner power, unless needed. Power should be <u>controlled</u> so one keeps a <u>peaceful state of mind</u>, unless when one is and/or feels threatened.
- Learn self and peace of mind, so one learns what situations one should remain in to maintain <u>safe</u> and <u>peace of mind</u>:
- <u>Stay relaxed</u> one has to prepare for the <u>future</u> not being able to change the past until we can change the past. When problems occur deal with them as much as one can and continue on. One must not beat one's self up, <u>unless one deserves it</u>. <u>Don't be so hard on yourself</u>. <u>Actions speak</u> louder than words. Become self, know self, and live as self, and what self brings, live life.

Best for self and others. (<u>Mind, Body, Spirit</u>) <u>Heart</u>

- Try to keep <u>body</u> from <u>unwanted</u> and/or <u>harmful</u>
- Maintain bacteria, infections, toxins, waste, and any other unwanted pests or parasites
- One shouldn't lose LOVE
- One must try to see the <u>good in all</u> and let it flow. Stay balanced
- One should always value loyalty, honest, respect in all kind.
- One shouldn't <u>blame someone</u> for an <u>action</u> that <u>wasn't committed</u>. (Don't kill the messenger)
- One should keep the eyes open, you never know the <u>answer</u> could be right in front of your nose. Be <u>open minded</u>, and finding the answer is <u>possible</u>.
- One shouldn't judge a person are creature too quickly. One might miss out on a good thing.
- Hatred will always be around, one must stay focused on ones goals and not let the hate sink in or push one off balance
- <u>One shouldn't have to prove anything to someone other than self</u>, unless that person has proven to be respectful
- <u>One shouldn't let obstacles</u> stop them from completing a set task and/or action.

- Action should be true and honest done to please self-more than others unless otherwise needed.
- One shouldn't let hate seep into one heart this can turn ones heart very cold.
- Take things for what they are and not what was intended to be. (What is, is what is until it isn't)
- <u>Live</u> life in <u>peace</u> with a <u>peaceful piece of mind</u>, <u>balanced</u> and <u>centered</u> at all times when possible, and remember that no one is <u>perfect</u>, but one can reach one own <u>perfection</u>.
- People lie, cheat, and steal to get what they want and need. One can't really know another person truly one can truly know self, unless one lets you into their world.
- One should learn one's body inside and out to better known one's self and other to better understand life.
- A friend of a friend is a friend unless that friend's friend is an enemy.
- An enemy's, enemy is a possible friend, unless that enemies enemy is an enemy.
- Sometimes it's better to listen and learn rather than act. One must make the wisest actions if one what's to succeed. Stay focus and absorb what is and not what isn't. Sometimes a friend will look like an enemy because of one's situation when really it is <u>one's mind</u> that has <u>become</u> the enemy. Make the <u>wisest choices</u> by being wise, and knowing <u>what is</u> and <u>what isn't</u>. If one makes the <u>wrong choice</u> then <u>one may fail</u> and <u>meet</u> <u>defeat</u>. In order to win one must know who is friend and who is foe, separate the real from the unreal and then one can make <u>the wisest choice</u>.
- Sometimes <u>in the mist</u> <u>of battel</u> one should take a step back a really see what is happening without the worry of action or threat.
- Better to walk away from a fight than to make an unwanted situation escalate to something that could possibly take one's life.
- Learn to move as a sphere, having no limitation, to self-movements no limits.
- In order become what's wanted one must practice being what wanted
- <u>Balance</u> is give and take, must find the center and <u>blame</u> self.
- Its all in the way you look at things you see what you want to <u>see</u>.
- One shouldn't judge others until one has first judged one's self.

- Never expecting someone else to act like you let them be them.
- Power is what you make it and nothing more.
- One must be wise when using ones power.
- The truth will clear the mind conscience and free the mind of what is false. Best for one to be rueful. (Useful knowledge is always useful)
- Find what is TRUE to self
- Write a section about the art of throwing opponents
- <u>Dodge ball</u> is also a great fun to practicing the state of untouchableness, gaining skill in eye body <u>coordination</u> and agility. Try not to be hit or/and practice being untouched. <u>Dodge ball</u> a game played by usually two or more persons, someone <u>throwing</u> ball, and somebody <u>dodging</u> the ball. Use able try using learned techniques and learn some new ones keep track of new movements even if you note them mentally. (Perfection takes practice)
- <u>Foundation</u> each limb has its own foundation learn the range for each limb to learn self.
- One should ask one's self: If one is inside in a place of dwelling, is one just one or is one (one + dwelling)? These are the questions one should ask self to better find self. Can one be only one or more than one?
- It takes more than one to raise a village together we stand strong like a great herd of elephants. Try your best to stick to your morals <u>practice</u> and <u>practice</u>, some more any progress is good progress.
- Jumping drills for agility one leg at a time while keeping your balance on one leg, kick them

Jump on other leg kick, and then repeat while keeping balance, this will help with agility and burst kicking and overall kicking speed. Try to switch to the next leg as quick as possible like hot leg or hot potato. Have fun when practicing make drills and practice fun, so training will be more likely to be carried out because it's an activity that you like to do. Make it as fun as possible. And the possibility of it happening becomes greater. Train to become perfection even though nothing perfect. >>

- <u>Running</u> and <u>walking</u> helps with <u>agility</u>, helps <u>to keep balance through different actions while going through actions</u>.
- One should keep his /or her balance through the body movements,
- Stay in your relax state unless <u>anger</u> and controlled <u>aggression</u> is needed.
- Maintain untouchable state as long as possible and once someone enters defend and then return to untouchable state once opponent has been taking care of. Fighting should be the last resort in self-defense.

<u>Agility Training + Drills + Cardio</u>

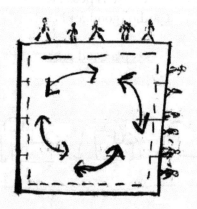

side to side building up the legs
Leg over leg moving sideways building speed & power

This is best done in an area with enough room to freely do the exercise.
The faster the better, keep balance during each exercise
Make sure each one exercise is done properly.

Tires training

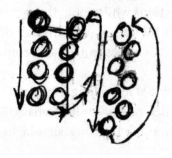

Box jumping
As fast as possible
Cardio (good for heart)

Keep a good pace

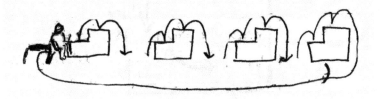

Box jumping
Jumping to build
Legs + calves

Make sure balance is kept through the whole exercise. Keep knees bent and keep hands in front in case you have to catch yourself, and to help keep balance.

* Obstacle training is very effective when training for agility, and learning the untouchable state.

• Jump rope is another great agility workout, but make sure your rope is long enough.

Both legs, and once you get better try one leg at a time. Take your time keep balance and focus on balance while in motion while balance changes from one leg to another.

To be the best you can be, you must first train like the best, to be the best. Step higher, when ready, don't limit self.

- Knowing one's own ability is very helpful when training to be ones best. Find self and become one.
- When exercising your neck and arms & back there are many exercises but I like these one

Keep legs pointed to the sky and hold this position as long as you can, try lifting your body if possible towards the sky, once muscles are strong enough, do vertical push up, this will build the arms, las, delta, back. This will also help to maintain full body balance. If you are unable to do this, try using a wall to help keep your legs up, or a workout partner to spot you. Be very careful not to injury yourself, when finish raise slowly to feet let the blood flow back through the body. If you don't you may faint due to loss off oxygen to the brain. Keep good circulation

- Shouldn't smoke during training, this way the body will be able to take in more air stronger lungs.
- Everyday life outside of matches should be pleasant and calm, learning from experienced, sitting in a dark room and go over the match in a mental state, learning from each match. Keep normal life separate from matches and remain self.
- Don't let anyone take you out of your state of calmness. People talk, don't let it eat you up. If you do they win, and you will end up with unwanted anger and aggression, try to remain cool like a running stream, smooth like silk, but as hard as iron. Keep relax state and keep balance and focus. Sometimes more than not taking deep breaths to ease self and self-state of mind. Control self even when you feel uncontrollable. Inner Peace: Contain the inner energy, or inner beast or inner animal and channel it through another actions, self-control.

- Sometimes it's <u>better</u> to walk away, rather than harm or be harmed, stay relaxed and <u>focus</u> on <u>one's</u> <u>life</u>, and <u>balance</u> in <u>one's</u> <u>life</u>. When you feel <u>unwanted anger and aggression</u>, one should think about something other than the situation that is causing the anger and aggression. Stay relaxed and walk away unless you are unable to.
- Each limb has its pivot, different limits or/and boundaries for each limb. Find the limits boundary and/or range for each limb.

<u>Learn your flower</u>: Pivots for each limb. (Mind over matter, pain no only <u>action</u> until there's no action.) Learn self totally and fully learn what you like and what feel comfortable. Fix if fixable, don't limit self. Find limits and break them down, if you can't reach the top by yourself, find help or other tools to complete actions. Don't be afraid or ashamed to ask for help. Of course not during combat, during regular, normal everyday life. Break down limits in self to find whole one must know self to understand life. Life should be simple, and sweet with some bitter spots, and seeds. Focus on progress no matter what it is any progress is good progress. Don't let yourself get in your way. Find a path and go for it. Nothing is perfect, but that's life. Can't live without it.

- When back is against the wall you have actually closed a few lines of danger, but you also have less room to maneuver, must be quick with actions at this time. If possible, use your opponent's weight, force, and/or balance against them. Make sure each technique counts, even if it's to throw off your opponents eyes, weight, force and/or balance.

Shouldn't fight a fight you can't win, unless given <u>no other choice</u>. One should also search for peace. Build body for <u>speed</u>, <u>agility</u>, <u>balance</u>, and <u>power</u>. Keep practicing burst, punches, and burst kicks. Usually if you beat the biggest or majority usually you won't have to worry about the rest when dealing with more than one opponent. Take care of the rest of opponent with a clear mind. Never underestimate your opponent or opponents. Always having mind and eyes open. Ready to blend in or mold together with opponent or opponents. <u>Focus</u>!!! Untouched until they enter the realm.

- Keep balance through each action and focus on your targets at all times while in fight mode.

Never enter a battle knowing victory, tides change quickly. Never underestimate your opponent, or you will give your opponent an advantage during the match, you might meet an unwanted surprise. Keep head up eyes open and focus on your opponent, once again read your opponent and plan your opponent's next move. Muscle tension helps when looking for a tale tail sign for an opponent's quick release, or/and action.

- Sometimes it's not the action what happen, it's what happens after the action that matters most. Stay focus and aware of environment, with mind clear.
- Find the beat to the match and then find/feel the beat within self.
- Always better to be safe than sorry so no accident happen. But no one's perfect.
- Better to say sorry for disrespecting than to have an altercation. Better to control the anger and aggression than to let it overwhelm. Remember to try and stay relaxed.
- Don't let pride or ego get in the way, what is, is and will be that way until what is changes. Control power don't let overwhelm.

Leverage

Leverage usually plays the biggest factor when in close range hand to hand combat. You must to be able to or train to be able to bend the match to your favor. Balance also play an important role in Leverage gaining, the upper hand in the match. Usually, first hits win when dealing with burst throwers (Feet hands) Once the blows are thrown they shouldn't stop until the match is over. Other techniques should also be applied. When in combat play to win, with the respect for life.

- Learn how to read your opponent and react before they respond. Learn your and your opponent's personal space and take advantage of the time given, by opponent.

- How long can one win be the best you can be and then keep bettering yourself progress is always good don't limit self or you'll stunt self-growth.

Be <u>boundless</u> and <u>anything</u> is <u>possible</u>. Free

- Maintain an <u>untouchable state</u> as often as possible unless in the realm of the opponent.

Empty space

Untouched state
Simple = genius
Simplest form
Simplified abs =c
If you can't teach; then I untouched

- Life will get hard, and then harder leaving one callused, better experienced, and better skill, giving one a better way of living life, as long as one can cope with the stress and strain of life.
- It is better for one to say nothing, then to say a lot of nothing
- One should never take life for granted, life is precious and should never be overlooked because without life there is only death.
- It is best to clean the body at least once a day ridding the body of toxins, and dirt and oil that suffocate the body clogging the pores, this will bring vitality and a new outlook on life and bring forth positive energy, after the day has been cleansed and the body has been cleaned in with positive energy, out with negative energy. Keeping the mind, body, and spirit free from contamination. Daily bathing also helps in cleaning the sinuses, giving one power in action and mobility greater.
- Apply vitamins and moisturizers to moisten the skin to help the body rid itself from infection and disease. This should be done daily for best results. Giving the body a great healthy glow. Making one feel better the body energizing
- One should also shave as often as possible and keep the body and mind fit vitamins and other medicines will help in this area. One's health is key to one's survival.
- One should not need to take what is not yours. One should be able to sustain life by one's own means to live and prosper, because one wouldn't want someone taking from them, it is said it is best to treat others as if they were self, this creates positive karma
- One shouldn't borrow more than one can return this also creates positive karma and helps one build bonds that may become helpful in the future.
- One should never point the finger at the innocent it is always best to point the finger in the direction of the one responsible, separating fact from fiction, is the way to a strong mind.
- When one becomes surrounded by grief and despair and does not know which way to turn or which step to take next, it is best to keep moving forward, until one finds a better path.
- Beware the knowledge you share with other, for the can become stronger then thy teacher. (Knowledge is power)

- Some of the best physical training lies within the minds of athletes, athletes
- To manage one's anger one must place one's anger in the correct place in the correct manner, to reframe from, letting one's anger take control, anger can be one's must deadliest friend
- Life teaches life to live life, (pay close attention to the lessons of life to survive the tests of life).
- One must learn to become better than men. (Life will show the way).
- Attraction can be a positive or a negative action

Explain -   - peace - power
             - Knowledge and

- The way to enlightenment, is the way of the dragon. I hope I've been helpful in helping you find your way.

- In the mist of battle one must look at one's self as a predator, never prey. This predatory state of mind will change the way you look at your opponent. This predatory state of mind will also increase one's confidence within battle.

- It is belief that drive a man, guiding one to do what seems to be right and just, (The greatest power in the universe is BELIEF) (One must belief to ???)

Denser muscle will increase the amount of power per square inch p.m. chi will increase ones density, concentrated muscle tone.

- No love can come from hate
- The final test of man will be the fight with life because there will be no fight from death.
- The ability to protect or fight is a great skill but to love is the greatest ability of all cherish one's self and one loved ones for one never knows how long we will last.
- A man grows from boy to man, hiding the beast within, once one has learned to control one's self one must master the beast within. But to become whole, one must become one with self and one's inner being, maintain a constancy mental frame, cool calm, and collective

while controlling both man, and beast, yin and yang, soft and hard, only then will one be able to reach enlightenment.

- Gender doesn't matter in the eyes of combat, leverage is the most valuable piece of the combat puzzle, gender plays no role in combat for the Tigris with cub can become more treating the male tiger, because of her instinct to protect her young.
- One must learn to control ones anger especially when ones anger becomes strongest. Learn to redirect one's anger turning into something positive, (turning ones negativity into something positive.) In order to become a great martial artist <u>one must be just and righteous</u> forever <u>controlling</u> the beast within.
- Put a sword in the hand of the enemy and one stands a great chance of being beheaded but a sword in the hands of a friend becomes another source of protection, one must???
- If one doesn't have love for one's teacher or ones students ones art will become tainted with negative energy which will produce hatred for others. Which will turn life against self it is best to show compassion for ones fellow man.
- <u>One must remain disciplined</u>
- I admire and respect the lion, but the lion would eat me as well as you. Take life for what it is unless you are willing to change what life is.
- Knowledge of self is the root to happiness. One must know what happiness is in order to find happiness. There is still love in this world, one only has to find it, and hatred can't be???
- In order to destroy the beast one must first destroy the heart of the beast and then attack until every breath of the beast has seize to exist destroy the beast from the inside out.
- One should protect what is most valuable to self.

(Adaptation is the key to motion, one must be able to move in and out of danger without getting harmed, moving without thought, moving without mind, changing with change at a moment's notice. Making your self-defense a natural reflex, reprogramming the mind body and spirit to act and move as one with thought without mind, one must be able to adapt to life it's self this requires much repetition and training, but once one has train one's body to adapt to movement, protecting one's self with no mind or thought, one will only have to live to survive.

- Martial arts should always be used to defend, used as a defensive way to stay alive and unharmed.
- Combat between self and one's opponent is the same, that is why it is best to truly understand what one is fighting for (love thy self, and understand thy enemy.) One should never love thy enemy for thy enemy will show no mercy in the heat of battle and/or combat.
- A person will believe almost anything you tell them, and take it as fact. This is programing someone's sub conscience to believe what you want them to believe. [Ex: tell somebody it is going to rain when it's not knowing that it isn't going to rain, and having that person believe that it is going to rain.] Believe what is true and if the knowledge is unknown research, and find out the truth.
- Training your conscience and subconscious mind (dragon) protection.
- Entity First one learns technique gaining skill and experience, learning how to protect self, programming the conscience and subconscious mind, then once one has train enough ones subconscious state of mind becomes strong in defense and action this is what some call the (dragon) Once one has reached this level in spirit, mind, and body (3) One must then train to control ones dragon or subconscious state of mind while also controlling on conscience state of mind once again the yin and yang takes place the balance in life.

Strengthening ones dragon requires great skill, determination, patience, practice, and experience, one can always increase ones skill and experience in spirit, mind, and body, (open one's eyes to life.) One must never give up

Increase ones skill and raise ones level

- If possible one should never travel alone, strength is greater in numbers.
- Never surround one's self with who wish harm of one's self.
- It is always good to keep a means of protection on one's person, in case one needs to protect one's self.
- One should never start offensive altercation, one only defend one's life, and loved ones. Fighting should never become the answer.
- It is best to show humility, even when one contains the upper hand. (Peace is always the answer to chaos)
- One should always keep a constant mental note of ones state of mind, and anger, and aggression level in order to act
- Hearing something and understanding what you've heard is two completely different things, to truly understand what one hears, one has to understand what one has heard. Sometimes one must listening in repetition, (many times over) to truly understand the meaning of what is heard. Programming the subconscious mind to hold onto what is learned, making this new knowledge necessary to the mind.

<u>Softwood</u> - ??? To strengthen and harden the shin foot, and other parts of the lower body, one can also use hand techniques as well, strengthening the body by striking the wooden post using the techniques learned, wrap a cushion around the post until one's body grows accustomed to the hardness of the post.

$$\boxed{\text{Repetition}}$$

- Progress Chart - added to book needed

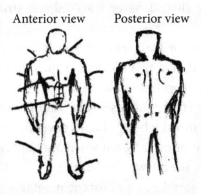

Anterior view   Posterior view

Example: January

Monday	Tuesday	Wednesday	Thursday	Friday	Saturday	Sunday	

- Anterior (front)
- Posterior (back)
<u>Views</u> of body

- Mark down the progress of each muscle and/or muscle groups sets to understand the status of one's <u>body</u>, write down the pros, and cons of one's body and improve, change, and sculpt one's body into ones ideal image

??? Slight misjudgment of one's mental state, or aggression level can cause one to react unwisely which in some cases can be harmful to one's self, and others. (Always be aware of one's present state of mind).

- One must <u>truly love</u> one self, and ones loved ones, and make righteous decisions. It is best to make decisions with a clear neutral state of mind.
- Neutral states of mind reveals what is true in nature, and life.
- <u>Progress</u> is always a key to unlock the doors of the future.
- Remember that hatred can blind even the wisest of men.
- <u>Self-control is the key to life.</u>
- A great martial artist <u>should</u> never have to use ones abilities to fight.

Monday
100 push ups
100 sit ups
30 min weight training
10-20 min run or jog

Progress	Goal
80 to 100 push up	200 push ups
80 to 100 sit up	200 sit ups
100 pounds max	200 max

Note needs more room for writing

Horse Stance

More info
More detail and depth
[One should never be afraid to go back to the beginning]
Progress is key

- Horse Stance and all other stances builds strength within the body, ankles, feet, legs, gluts, abs and many other parts of the body, creating balance, and balance in motion.
- There is always more to life then the eye can see, there is always much more to the story, then what you hear, reality was once fiction, until the day of true. One must separate fact from fiction, to truly understand what truth really is, and to realize what life is, and what life can become remember any is possible, all one needs in life is the answers to the problems of life, applying the answers to life's problems is always left up to the ones who gain the knowledge of life, the answers to life makes life less confusing and more often than not, easier to manage or control.

(Time + Dedication + Practice) = Progress

As one practices, and trains to move in and out of one's stance together with technique, creating focus, concentration power and energy, strengthening one chi, having a lower center of gravity creates a stronger posture and denser muscle mass, making it easier to remain in stance and motion, these muscles must remain strong, just like every other part of one's body. One's stance must feel comfortable, and useful strong and noble, so one can move freely in and out of one's stance, pay close attention to the balance, and posture of the body, and pay extremely close attention to the balance and position of the feet, because one can maneuver around any obstacle and defeat any attack with <u>footwork</u>.

<u>Theory</u>

If you can imagine something, then in theory whatever is imagined can be brought to life, one only has to dream, and (find the equation, and solve the problem to find the answer).

- If you can imagine something, then in theory whatever one imagined can be brought to life, one only has to dream. (Find the equation to ones problems in life, and solve ones problems to find the answers of life).
- The eyes see what lie on the surface of truth, but the true meaning of the truth lies buried beneath what one's eyes can see. (Read between the lines of illusions of life to find what truth really is) (Beneath the mirror image lie true meaning of life).
- There is always more to life then the eye can see, there is always much more to the story, then what you hear, reality was once fiction, until the day of true. One must separate fact from fiction, to truly understand what truth really is, and to realize what life is, and what life can become remember any is possible, <u>all one needs in life is the answers to the problems of life</u> applying the answers to life's problems is always left up to the ones who gain the knowledge of life, the answers to life makes life less confusing, and more often than not, easier to manage or control.

(Time + Dedication + Practice) = Progress

06-10-12

- One must remember there are no guarantees in life, people lie, and accidents happen. (Trust thy self)
- One should always remain grateful and cherish all of the treasures that life may bring.
- A dragon that sees all doesn't necessary know all, life is an illusion the surface of what is, to gain true knowledge one must venture beyond what is seen.
- It is one thing to learn, but to practice what one learns is a totally different world, (practice what one learns, and learn to teach)
- One can get inside the head of ones opponent by bring down ones opponents self-esteem by insulting ones opponents abilities, making ones opponent's ability feeling enactiquet inactiquet enactiquet, this ability will create confusion, leaving ones opponent feeling uneasy, and unbalanced, creating actions from ignorance instead of wisdom, creating more opportunity for action. This is the perfect opportunity for one to act. (One must always, be aware of attack, keeping ones guard up in case
- Expect nothing and one will have no disappointments in life, expect everything, and life will be forever disappointing (nothing in life is guaranteed)
- One should close as many lines of attack as possible, making blocks, counters, and attacks easier to do. By closing lines of attacks or lines of danger one will be able to block, counter with extremely less time, waiting for one opponents actions to spring to life, practicing closing the lines of attacks or lines of danger in repetition will build the mind, body, and all of ones senses and will reprogram the mind to act without thought, acting without mind or ones active conscience this is training the mind subconscious state where the long term memory lies.
- If one doesn't practice the teachings of life, ones skills will soften, and grow weak. It is best to strengthen and perfect one skills and abilities in life, and watch ones skills and abilities bloom, these are the words of the wise).

(Practice + skill + experience)^2 = greatness

- Never let ones confidence and knowledge of self-exceed ones safety

- Beware the competition of two when there is only room fit for one, for competition can turn to war (look for the patterns in life to foresee the truth in ones future).

- Becoming different doesn't necessarily mean one is better, or greater than, being different means that one is not the same. It is always best to be, or become one's self while creating what is truly to self

- The world is filled with much hate, and hatred, it is key to become the opposite of this (hatred), hatred breeds jealousy, envy, sickness, and death, enemies, and foes (Be careful

- Search for truth, understanding, wisdom, peace, and peace of mind, enlightenment, focus, and spirituality in life to help guide one's self to one's own path. The path of righteousness, search for the path of truth.

- Beware friendly altercations, for play can turn in to fights within an instant. To avoid this, keep a watchful eye on the emotional state of one's opponent.

Sometimes the winds lie. It is best to consider the facts of life and truly judge for one's self, testing the winds like life. One must truly see what is, and what isn't in order to find what is true, because sometimes the winds lie.

- One should learn one's own patterns in life, training to change these patterns, when necessary at will when need be. This will help one's <u>ability</u> to foresee ones future, as long??? Pattern.
- Wise men say to show mercy, but only to those who truly deserves, or those who need to be saved. Keep a watchful eye on those who have been shown mercy for they, may not return the favor
- The objective in martial arts is to protect life and others and defend one's life when needed, and to find ones path to spirituality and enlightenment and many other thing. Martial art is not for bulling or the projection or harm, (for peace never chaos).

- If you can image something, then in theory whatever one imagined can be brought to life, one only has to dream. (Find the equation to ones problems in life, and solve ones problems to find the answers of life).
- The eyes see what lie on the surface of truth, but the true meaning of the truth lies buried beneath what one's eyes can see. (Read between the lines of illusions of life to find what truth really is) (Beneath the mirror image lie true meaning of life).
- Becoming different doesn't necessarily mean one is better or greater than, being different means that one is not the same. It is always best to be, or become one's self while creating what is true to self

- The world is filled with much hate, and hatred, it is key to become the opposite of this (hatred)???

Can be positive if one chooses to use ones art in a positive manner, but ones art can also be used in a negative manner depending on how one uses ones abilities. The path of energy totally depends on you. One should always stay balanced and seek the righteous of path and live in the greatest light of peace, never surrounding one's self with chaos and destruction.

- When one is surrounded by hatred, and feels like there is nothing one can do, one must then love one's self and one's own beliefs more than anyone else can ever do, in turn this will raise ones confidence and one's self value. Increasing ones inner peace.
- A great way to find out if one is truly friend, one should test ones friends by playing the friendship game, (back starching) if one shares a cold drink with a friend, then if ones friend is truly a friend, one's friend would then in turn share a drink, this is a great test to see if one truly cares or if ones friend just wants to take advantage (if one surrounds self with people who just take one will end up with nothing)
- The objective in self-defense is to???

One should stay as wild as possible without getting one's self into trouble learning what life is like outside the box, like the indoor cat that has nothing but friends us, the outside cat that app???

- Sometimes to create something new one must think outside the box, outside of what is normal or what is known. One should find one's own path to find ones true self.

- You can give a man a sword, but that doesn't mean that, that man knows the correct way would or use a sword. One must teach ones student the correct way of the sword, one must teach ones student the way to the righteous path.
- One should never let hatred consume oneself whole, hatred is a human emotion and can destroy anything and everything that it comes in contact with seeping through the heart and mind crapping out through the soul or pores of self-creating a different being,

this is the birth place of chaos, instead of consuming hatred whole one must find a way to transform this hatred into something else, something great and good, like a tree that releases seeds after a great fire creating life from death, heaven out of hell hatred is the destroyer of life, and must be eliminated in order to bring forth order and peace in times of war and chaos transform ones hate into something better than hate, transform ones hate into peace *(Theirs is a solution to every problem one only has to find the way) *Survival is key*

- Martial Arts is not about combat and conflict martial arts is the ability to live a peace existence with fighting, and avoid conflict. (Peace is always the answer.)
- Believe in one's self, and ones beliefs, and one will gain one of life's truest powers. One should never stop believing.

- Life is like two hands, what is true for the right hand, is not always true for the left hand, even though they both connected to the whole. Each situation is different, so one must take each situation in life as a new creation, or a new situation, dealing with each new situation like the beginning of life, soaking in any, and all knowledge determining what is true for self. (Create a new beginning and believe in one self, and ones abilities) (Never give up)

Protect one's self, to do this one must be able to defend one's self against attack, a great martial arts can defend self while remaining untouched, staying out of the line or range of danger, by blocking dodging and countering one's opponents attack or offensive actions. This requires much training and discipline. One must train the mind, body, and spirit to act as a whole, to be able to act and react without thought or doubt, to train one's eyes and mind to see what is, and what will be, this is only possible with great training and time. Practice practice practice

- Using the elements of life to one's advantage, or absorbing energy from the elements, and letting the elements work for you, the sun, wind, water, earth metals, and any other force of nature that may come in handy. These forces are real, and remain constant, and extremely powerful, using the senses and forces of nature, with one's mind, body, and spirit will increase ones energy level, which in turn will increase ones power, like throwing a stone into a pond changing the shape of the water, like the <u>rains</u> turning into rivers, strong enough to crush even the strongest of men like the wind in its most common form??? Mind???

- The answer to a problem is always the best answer. The solution to a problem is always the best solution, if one does not know the answer or solution to a problem one can always ask.

- <u>Complexity</u> is not the answer to ones problems, simplicity is <u>complexity</u> is the way to solve ones answers, to ones problems or equations in life, and <u>simplicity is the answer</u>. One must simplify to find one answer to complexity.

- <u>Windmill and stand</u> research the and find the name of the ball with to ropes at each end and add to, find more train devices (like a tether ball)

- Training pillar (single) with rope or padded canvas buried in about a foot below ground, standing one foot over head

- Weight bench, and anything else that will help in your martial way

The hands of man can move the earth, a man's spirit can move mountains, and water to seed brings fourth life of tree which in turn brings fourth food for life. Fire can bring fourth the end to life, or energy for life, the warmth of the flame which warms the soul, fire is great energy, and should be respected highly in the world of martial arts, a brief absence of mind gives this element the opportunity to take life, this is why this element should be controlled more ??? The angry???

Punches

Jab

Hook

Cross

Straight

Upper cuts

Quarter punch

Back first

Elbows

Front elbow

Rear elbow

Side elbow

Upper elbow

Kicks knees

Front snap kicks

Side kicks

Ax kicks

Spin kicks

Sweeps

Jump kicks

Front-step-in kick

Rear kicks

Blocks

Hands

Feet

Elbow

Forearm

Shoulders

Knees

- <u>Beware the selfishness in others</u>. Those who remain selfish, will turn on you when it suits them. This usually happens when one lease expects, usually when one's eyes are closed to the truths of life, when one has reached ones weakest point. This is usually the strongest point of attack or intrusion for one's enemy, when leverage is the opposing side, weaker for
- A man covered in blood pleading for peace is to be highly respected because he is the one who holds the sword. (Peace is never to be considered weakness, <u>a peaceful existence is what greatness is</u>).
- One should find <u>laughter</u> in <u>humility</u>, <u>peace</u> out of <u>chaos</u>, <u>happiness in sadness</u>, and <u>love</u> out of <u>hate</u>. <u>Learn</u> yourself truly and one will gain the <u>ability</u> to control
- Be aware those who try to take what's closest to you.
- Mass, weight, pressure, and momentum will increase the <u>pounds per square inch</u>, (keep in mind the human body can be destroyed with nothing but pressure, and increase the amount of pressure and one will increase the amount of damage). One must learn how to control the amount of pressure applied during each action. To reach a better sense of being
- A wise man should never leave a treasure unveiled. One must protect what is valued most.
- Remember to keep a slightly bent knee for better balance and range of motion in motion. (Through each technique to add better balance and power through action).
- The most important key to winning is to <u>win</u>, size shape height, or weight make no guarantees & usually the best fighter wins, unless ones opponent finds a way to tip the scales in their favor the only option to winning is to win. (It's the size of the fight in the dog.)
- Find the ability to make self-happy and always love yourself no matter what

Never give up, and strive to become great (<u>Never give up</u>.)

- (To understand the mood of the lion one must first look into the eyes of the lion, only then will you truly understand what a lion is.)

- Always remember a true friend is the one to help you up when you fall not the one who laughs because you fell, even if the one who helps you up laughs as well. The true friend is the one who??? You off and helps you???

This creates a greater chance for success. (Study thy enemy)

- When all the senses become unreliable, one must separate life's illusions from reality to find truth. Life is full of illusion (<u>truth</u> and <u>honesty</u> will show the way to the realities of life). <u>Wisdom</u>, <u>trial</u> and <u>error</u> is <u>the key to truth</u>

Truth is knowledge

Life brings your way,
- Only surround self with peace, love, loyalty and happiness to do this must first be free from one self from hate.
- Always help the ones who help you, because the ones who care the most are most important in friendship.
- The objective is to enter the realm of another's personal space, and controlling their space, and energy, plus one's own space and energy. Making room???

One's emotions, one should make the best out of each and every situation, no matter what the situation may be, one must truly find <u>happiness</u> and <u>peace</u>, by living a truly peaceful existence.

- Meditation and positive energy will decrease stress and create a better positive outlook to life. Keep peace over chaos to help keep the negative energy from <u>interfering</u> with one's life.

<u>So much to learn</u>
*baby step to success is the key to success!

One must practice
Making ones opponent space one's own, making the space around safe and clear from attack, blocking and countering anything and everything that gets in the way, (practice blocking counterattacks, and invading ones opponents actions, within the circle of ones opponent

while protecting self at all times.) This practice is vital to one's self defense one must practice, practice, and practice

(Practice + repetition + time + accuracy) = skill

It's because of the things in life that bother them, carrying the burdens and pouring them onto closest just to make their self-feel better, this is an unjust and unfair release of tension. (One should always remain in control of one's temper. Learn to control ones anger no matter what the situation is. Anger, love, hate, and fear can cause one to make the wrong decisions. Learn to control ones??? Situation in order???

One's emotions, one should??? The best out of each and every situation, no matter what the situation may be. One must truly find <u>happiness</u> and <u>peace</u>, by living a truly peaceful existence.

- Meditation and positive energy will decrease stress and create a better positive outlook to life. Keep peace over chaos to help keep the negative energy from <u>interfering</u> with one's life.

<u>So much to learn</u>

*baby steps to success is the key to success!

- The most important key to winning is to <u>win</u>, size, shape height, or weight make no guarantees. Usually the best fighter wins, unless ones opponent finds a way to tip the scales in their favor. The only option to winning is to win. (It's the size of the fight in the dog.)
- Find the ability to make self-happy and always love yourself no matter what
- Sometimes it is better to go through the bush, rather than around it. The shortest distance from point A to point B is a straight line. One may have many obstacles in the way of one's path, but every obstacle can be moved or??? Change??? For success. ???
- When all the senses beck??? Unreliable, one must separate life's illusions from real??? To find truth. Life is full of illusion (<u>truth honesty</u> will show the??? to the realities of life). <u>Wisdom, trial,</u> and??? Is <u>the key to trust</u>? Truth is knowledge.

One must practice

Making ones opponent space one's own, making the space around safe, and clear from attack, blocking and countering anything and everything that gets in the way, (practice blocking counterattacks, and invading ones opponents actions, within the circle of ones opponent while protect??? self at all times.) This practice is vital to one's self defense one must practice, practice, and practice

(Practice + repetition + t??? + Accuracy) = Skill

- It is best not to look for reasons to hate someone, instead it is best to search for reasons to bond with others, search for the common ground between the lines of difference, (one never knows what one will find between the lines of difference.)
- It is okay to make fun of one's self, because ones mistakes should be pointed out in order to make progress, to better right a wrong.
- Before making important decisions, one should sit back and remain in deep thought before jumping forward with action to keep self from making the wrong decision. (Think first about ones actions before one makes the wrong decision so ones heart doesn't become full of regret. It is best to make decisions from a neutral position, with a righteous and just state of mind. (Find the information needed before action.)
- It is always best to live a life without doubt, enemies, negativity, and regret. It is best to surround self with positive energy. This way of life will lessen the stress that comes with life. When one lives by the gun, one risks the chance of dying by the gun. Eliminate every threat to life, and one will live a true life of peace, harmony, and peace of mind, with no worries. This is the kind of life I find in my dreams (one???
- Never take your eyes off the fight in the heat of battle. Battles can be won or lost in the blink of an eye
- If one ever has a problem in life, search for the answer, and never be afraid to ask for help, or advice from others, and remember there is no such thing as a dumb question, search for the truth and you shall

- One must seek advancement to make progress.
- One must step up to advance (to make progress) It is best to conceal ones true abilities, or to use the least amount of energy possible to win.
- If one know what if on the side of the mist

There are many paths to enlightenment, the path and choice of life style depends on you. A peaceful existence???

??? Mind in order to truly see what life is. (One must remain opened minded.)

- In order to change life one must change what is history.
- A family that plays together stay's together (surround yourself with love and loved ones.) Love is never wrong.
- There is much lost in life, one must learn to love and hold tight to what is most important
- Never felt sorry for shading tears for your fallen soldiers (Memories are everything, (never forget the ones you love.)
- Shouldn't blame others for one's own action, blaming others for one's own actions is a true lie to self, increasing the negativity in one's own life, truth should remain most important in life, or else you will live life as a lie, which is a true falsehood.
- One must find a way to become truth.

? and peace of mind;) Negativity will only bring one down, creating a life of chaos and depression, which is no way to live one must find peace and happiness within, and within life. (Become an object of peace not negativity.)

- Search for the beauty that lies within, (personality, and other characteristics, that??? find it.
- One should never worry about looking intelligent, one must first become intelligence, one shouldn't judge. One solely on appearance, study learn and observe to find the answer hidden within life.

One doesn't need to look through.

- A great mind will bring forth great wisdom and experience, use your wisdom wisely and great things will come your way
- It is best to search within for inner peace. It is best to stay calm and collective especially in stressful situations. Peace begins from within.

- If one surrounds one's self with negativity one receives negativity

If one surrounds one's self with positivity one receives positivity.

Less with threats to life create an opportunity to live a long and prospers life

- Imagine an idea, and bring it to life, like a rose from a seed, or a priceless painting. Created on a blank piece of canvas. (Never let your ideas, and dream escape you)

*Dream can come true. Dreams are the open windows of time, pay close attention to them, and never let them pass you bye. Dreams do come true.

- Peace should be the overall outcome in one's life, because in times of peace and times of war a true martial artist gains the power to feel the pain, pleasure, and stress and strain of others, this is the power of one: the ability to think, feel and be as one. This ability is greatly lessoned when ones angry and aggression has truly taking one over clouding the body and mind of one's true abilities in life, this feeling is a defense mechanism, do not let this feeling consume you entirely, one must maintain a calm and cool frame of mind to make the right decisions in one life preservation and protection of life is key.

<u>Eye of the dragon technique</u>

- Once one has obtained the ability of understanding what is truth, one will then be capable to walk through one's past and ???

02-08-2012

History creates the present, and one's past creates the future

- Because I can feel your pain. I shall not harm you, nor shall you harm me, one should always <u>teach</u> what is <u>righteous</u>, and <u>just</u> and <u>ensure</u> <u>peace</u> and <u>protection for all that live</u>.
- A man with a sword who wishes to harm all does not deserve to own such power, only those who respects life and others should be able to hold his sword, <u>chaos</u> is not the answer to those who love life.
- Let time becomes ones teacher testing ones morality and moral fiber life shall bring all the answers to every question in life. <u>Words from a wise man</u>.
- Sometimes in life one must mimic what is great or admired. Sometimes he must become something else in order to understand what is, like the man who watched the monkey in order to create the monkey styles, or the men of mantis who went North and South to create the mantis styles.
- In order to truly understand what is one must first become what is one can become whatever one wishes to be with time practice

<u>Repetition is the key!</u>

The past is already known

The future is unseen and containing unknown variable, when picking together one's future, one must choose the correct path in order to arrive at the correct location, as long as one sticks to the truth one's destination will remain, close if not exact to ones decided path. Truth is the key to the known and unknown

- Make a game out of it to obtain this ability ex: knowing how many steps it takes to get from A to B.
- Ones appearance should remain calm, and cool, even when it feels like the body is about to erupt, stay cool and calm like a lake with no ripples, smooth and pleasant like life should be, remember to remain calm.
- Life is the same no matter how you look at it, it is the choice one makes that determine good from bad but <u>life still remains the same</u>. (One should always think of life like it's and choose the correct path).

???

- Life can be very confusing at times, when one feels like one's life has gone astray, one must stick to what is truth, fantasy can lead one into some of the world's darkest of places, but fantasy or ones imagination can also bring forth life.
- One can redirect negative energy and turn this negative energy into some positive by changing the plan of action example: instead of choosing to pick a fight one should befriend, instead of starting a war, one should create peace of and peace of mind.
- Always listen to what is true and just this is the martial way. The way of life.
- When life becomes too heavy to hold, one can find peace and peace of mind within training the state of mind where there is nothing but one's self, a state of mind where the mind can free itself from worry and doubt in self, in order to be or live stress free one only has to rid one's self of stress

*life + stress = life
   <u>- Stress</u>
    Life = life

- There is no stress = there is just life.

- Fighting is not the most important part of fighting, presence is. A great fighter can win a fight with just presence alone, by presence I mean ones appearance and attitude, bringing ones opponent back to solid ground, get inside your opponents head and if one is trained properly one will gain the ability to talk ones opponent down, erasing the need or want, to fight, this takes much practice, and training, fighting should be the last choice of action. (<u>Defense is key</u>)

- <u>Like</u> any piece of protection, one should create control, or safety, like a sheath for a sword, built to control the power and strength that lies within, without this control one creates a higher probability for incident, control in key, create a sheath for your sword and use it to control the power that lies within.
- Times of <u>stress</u> and <u>depression</u> should be used to strengthen the mind, and inner child, by dealing with situation one cannot control, creating a stronger inner child and total being. (A stronger foundation)
- One should test one's ability to control ones anger and aggression, by first starting by <u>going a whole year without raising ones voice even in the most stressful of situations</u>, and continue to do so, each following year. Even though this test sounds easy enough, this <u>test</u> can sometimes break even the strongest of men. (One must remember that martial arts is just for protection, it must never be used to bully or???)
- Life is the taker of life, not death, death is the reliever of one's pain and suffering. Life is also the most precious thing in life. One must never take life for granted, one must live until the end, and rest until it is time to live again, energy never stops.
- One must find the formula to solve ones problems. If you can find the correct formula, one will gain the ability to solve any problem.
- The cure to ignorance is knowledge one must first learn to teach.
- Pick something to love, and continue to love this something for life, even after death, this is what is called unconditional love, in times to pleasure and times of pain, this is what true love is. One should also love one's self this way. (Learn what loyalty truly is). Never give up on what is loved. Ones love can be left unsaid, as long as ones action speak for self, but in times of stress and pain the word love can change the hearts of the savage.

- One should always keep what is sacred??? Hidden out of sight, in order to keep??? Is valued safe from harm? If??? One and opportunity to take what??? There's opportunity for one to do.
- Ones appearance should remain calm, and cool, even when it feels like the body is about to erupt, stay cool and calm like a lake with no ripples, smooth and pleasant like life should be, remember to remain calm.
- Life is the same no matter how you look at it, it is the choice one makes that determine good from bad but <u>life still remains the same</u>. (One should always think of life like this and choose the correct path).
- A lion is a lion no matter where the lion may roam.

A stronger foundation can keep a building standing even in the toughest of times. One must train one inner child to create a better whole.

- Why did the crocodile swim away from the hippo? Because the hippo would break the crocodile in half. (Preparation is key to fending off ones foes.) Always prepare to win.
- I train to defend self, training not to fight, but to defend one's life, becoming a better experience fighter is the outcome of this training, practice, practice, practice, (only bulls rush in)

$$(\text{Mind} + \text{body} + \text{soul}) = \underline{\text{freedom}}$$
$$\text{Life}$$

In one's art, one should notice that the eye for danger has increased, and ones movements and energy transfers become smoother in each action. (Just blocking and energy and balance transfer). *No offensive movements for six months to a year with this training, to open one's eyes for attacks.) The wooden dummy should help with this exercise greatly improving ones skills and ability in???

- To ensure life a fruit tree bear fruit, to appease the??? Wish to it eat, and instead of??? The whole tree, the tree fee??? Enemies fruit, and from??? Sacrifice the fruit tree is??? To reproduce, by feeding it's???

- <u>Sometimes one must feed in order to survive</u>, self s??? While maintaining one's own just a piece of fruit. (??? precious, and should be Val???
- Always listen to your body, and always give your body what it needs, eat when you need to, and always remain hydrated to help flush the body of unhealthy toxins.
- One must put one's own life first and foremost, to better preserve one's life, protect self and what is loved to maintain peace, violence should never be necessary. (Search for inner peace to find happiness.) (Without peace there's chaos)
- Greatness takes time, one should never give up hope, and one never give into failure??? Learn to win to win greatness and progress is the key, never give up hope, instead one must concentrate on making progress in one's own craft no matter what craft you practice. Never give up hope.
- Technique should start off with slow highly controlled movements, to better control ones movements within each technique, after a technique is learned, one must learn to control each techniques movement in stressful situation, in different angles, and positions, in and out of rhythm.
- It is better to die free then to live life as a slave.
- One must always know what one is capable of, to better increase the possibility of success.
- Know thy opponent like one should know thy enemy.
- War is a battle between differences of opinions that's all, and leverage is the key to success.
- Repetition will reprogram the brain and body to eat without thought, and without mind, practice is everything
- It is always best to be honest and just, (except in times of war.) <u>The only purpose of war is to win, there is no other option.</u>
- Shadows are reflection of the present, showing the motions of life, like the shadows of birds flying overhead, if one can see the shadows, one does not have to look overhead to see.
- Keep loose and ready for action until the moment of contact with target this will increase the amount of pressure for all actions.

- Power also comes for the opposite side of ones actions if one uses the right hand for attack, the energy for the left hand will increase the amount of pressure to one's action or attack
- The best peace is peace of mind.

<u>Inner peace</u>

- Envy turns to jealousy and jealousy turns to hatred, envy is opposite of the answer, when peace is the key. One should never be blinded by hatred.

<u>The choice is left up to you.</u>

The question is, why is hatred so powerful?

- This is why one must teach only what is true and lead one's students to the correct path, the path of peace and righteousness.
- I am just a reflection of energy that reflects upon me. Therefore I am truth.

To take advantage of an already existing opening, keeping a watchful eye open for any and all lines of ones opponents' action, one must learn to read the actions of one's self and one's opponent. (Remain untouched by any and all offensive action).

Stay Untouchable
Untouched

- When one trains a dragon, one must be careful in training, one never wants to enslave ones dragon, but instead one must teach ones dragon the righteous path, teaching right from wrong, this way ones dragon will become one's ally instead of one's enemy, if one enslaves ones dragon, ones dragon will have no choice but to rebel and naturally become ones bitter enemy. (One must teach ones dragon well). <u>The objective must always be to become better than one's self, this is called progress.</u>

- Always remain a safe distance from ones opponent until one feels comfortable to open up ones opponent for attack or???

Keys of Power

(What equals (power=)) add too later (remember the keys of power)

- Education
- Knowledge
- Love
- Experience
- Skill
- Patience
- Time
- Space
- Ability
- Hate
- Strength
- Fear
- Anger
- Determination
- Peace
- Confidence
- Ones will*
- Capability
- Respect
- Honor
- Loyalty
- Sexuality
- Compassion

(Brief description of each power)

*   *   *

- The best ones to teach

- Respect
- Listen
- Learn quickly
- And hold close a caring heart
- Loyalty is key training
- Natural ability
???
- Think of truth and speak the truth

Nervous System

<u>Graphs</u>

1. Mind
2. Body
3. Spirit
4. Strengthen Ones Total Being
5. Flower
6. Range of Motion
7. Human anatomy charts
8. Pressure points
   - Novice
   - Intermediate
   - Advance
9. More graphs to help progress
10. Most common vital point

***Expand: <u>Mind, Body, and Spirit Charts</u> more knowledge needed

<u>Mind</u>

Education, Writing, Reading, Training Knowledge, Repetition

<u>Body</u>

Exercise, Training Repetition

<u>(Spirit)</u>
Religion, Reading, Writing
(Energy)
(Presence)
(Aura)

To repeal what is disliked or unwanted one only has to rid one's self of
what is undesired, unlike or unwanted never allowing what is disliked,
to enter ones world, one must first find <u>leverage</u> to make this happen

expelling everything that is unwanted from one's life, keeping the undesired from entering ones circle of life or ones world, this will increase the positive flow for one's life, riding self of negative energy, creating peace for one's life and one's world, one must only add what is wanted if one wishes to control ones world. One can also change ones world at will by changing the pattern, equation, likes, dislikes, and desires of life, this can be done at any time as long as one contains the will to change what life is to one self. In order to attract the desires of life one must first become attractive to ones desires

- Once one has become attractive to ones desires, ones will have a better chance to attract ones desires

(One's life, experiences, environment, knowledge, likes, desires, dreams, dislikes, imagination, energy and everything that surrounds one life)

Pick your fights wisely

- A fight to prove who the best friend, ends up with a stronger friendship, is fighting over who's going to pay the bill.
- A fight to prove who the best is a combat can end in death
- The fight between love and hate will end in death for the innocent
- A fight that is blinded by hatred by both sides only ends in chaos.
- One should accept??? For what they are, and expect the unexpected change of character. (There is a pattern in all things, but patterns can change rapidly).
- Ones number one priority, should be one's faith and belief or beliefs, prioritizing this way will create one's own greatest path, or way of life, or way of living
- Cherish time every minute, and every second and remember materialistic things hold less value then love.
- The man that searches for freedom is the man who finds freedom

??? To practice

Techniques on pushing pad punching bag, wooden man, or just in an open space just as long as you practice.

To be underlined in close range hand to hand combat, you must be able to maintain your own space. You must be able to keep your opponent out of you circle.

Untouched
Touched

Once you commit to an action don't give your opponent time to react they might, will hit back, unless you maintain your untouched state.

To build the tools used for combat you need to practice and exercise each tool to complete its function. Reps are the best way to gain speed in a function, in close range hand to hand combat.

Martial Arts (Combat)

- Manage space between self and opponent.
- Try to keep total body balance. Try to keep legs under the body at all times. Keep a strong foundation the gloats are very helpful when flexed. Total body balance weather the weight is on the heal or the balls (front) of the feet. Most of the time its better to have a lower center of gravity.
- Knees should be bent slightly at all times unless when committed to an action.
- No matter the situation hydration always makes the body feel better and also helps cleans the body of waste.
- (Weight + Reps) = muscle tone
- Add more weight to increase muscle size.
- Range of motion is very important in combat, helps flexibility to complete each action.
- To increase power, you should start at the base of the body (feet) than bring that power and follow through to complete the action.
- Balance is always important in combat

Workout

More in depth workout try to warm up before to???

Cut through air

• Don't steal from me don't steal my thoughts

Bottom Half
Feet, calf, quads, hamstring, gluts, shine, legs etc.

Core, (Middle)
Front, and side abs, and lower back, last

Back
Upper, and lower back, muscles last, delta, neck muscles

Arms
Biceps, triceps, forearms, delta wrist, hand muscles
Concentrate on palms, and finger strength fingertips.
Chest: middle, top, bottom,

Cardio: lose calories and loss weight. (Cut weight)

Anything that speeds the heart up to produce sweet.
Running, jogging, sex, swimming, jump rope, stationary bike,
rollerblades, bike, jumping jacks, stairs, or just regular walking will
do just fine. The sauna is a great way to relief stress, and if you sweat
long enough you will also lose calories, and weight, while you burn
fat, you can see better muscle to me if there is let fat around the
muscle.

*Exercises muscle tone
Bottom Half (legs)
*Squats, leg press, leg curls

Core (Abs lower back)
*Sit ups, front and sides, last pull down. Ab scissors, etc.

Back: *Squats, *pushups, *bench pros, hand stands, military press,

Arms: *Hands - pushups on fingers, hand crunches
      *Biceps - curls (twist the dumbbell)
      *Triceps - reverse curls (tri pushdown) *Dips
      Forearms - straight arm curls
      Dolts - pushups, military press, let pull down
            Dumbbell raises

Chest: *pushups, *bench press, butterflies, work all sides of the chest
   (top, bottom, middle and sides)

      (Whole body)
Stretching: Legs, arms, back, neck, hands, feet, stomach
         (Whole body flexible) greater range of motion

Gloats

Cardio: Should be included into your workout routine to speed up the
   metabolism, to increase the amount of fat burned.

Muscle Tone: More repetitions in the set will increase muscle tone faster,
   the more sets of the reps the better.

Cut weight: for muscle building weight, reps +, sets, less calories
   consumed, heavy amounts of cardio healthy diet, visiting the sauna
   to keep sweating after cardio workout. A strong cardio workout, still
   keep to regular workout routine.

Printed in the United States
By Bookmasters